THE BUNKER DIARIES
BY STEWART MEYER

PUBLISHED BY BEATDOM BOOKS

Published by Beatdom Books

Copyright © 2025 by Stewart Meyer
Cover photograph by James Grauerholz

All rights reserved. No part of this book may be reproduced in any form or by any electronic or mechanical means including information storage and retrieval systems, without permission in writing from the author. The only exception is by a reviewer, who may quote short excerpts in a review.

ISBN: 978-1-0686980-1-9

First Print Edition

CONTENTS

1974.................................1
1978.................................5
1979................................27
1980...............................101
1981...............................145
1982...............................175
1983...............................207
INTERVIEW..........................219

INTRODUCTION
1974

I will never forget walking the long hallway of the English Department at City College in 1974 and coming to the door marked "WS Burroughs." Fearing paralysis, I quickly knocked. The door opened on a living legend and a very enlightening friendship...

I introduced myself and said it was an honor to meet him. He smiled and I was ushered into the small office and introduced to Burroughs' son, Billy. I'd just read his book, *Kentucky Ham*, about detoxing at the Federal Narcotics Farm in Kentucky. We talked a bit. I was too in awe of Burroughs to address him and was grateful for Billy's friendly chatter. He had tattoos, a few gold teeth, and a diddy-bop haircut.

On the way to class I walked behind Burroughs, looking at the attaché case he carried and thinking, "He's got The Word in there."

The classroom was packed. Burroughs did not take attendance. He sat down, pulled typed notes out of his attaché, and began to read. The classroom situation placed no attention on me. I was free to observe. Burroughs spent the entire class on the light at the end of Daisy's dock in *The Great Gatsby*.

The class ended and I wondered what to do. Could I approach him? Should I just beat it and digest the situation? Maybe wait until the next class. I did not want to blow this opportunity. Before I could even begin to form a strategy, Mr. Burroughs approached me and said, "Are you going downtown?"

"Yes. I have a car down the hill. Can I give you a ride?"

He smiled and said, "Let's go."

We walked out of the campus and down the slope to my old VW Bug. Settling in, he saw the fat roach I'd been smoking in the ashtray. "Smells good in here," he said.

"Light it."

"Let's get away from campus first."

We rolled downtown toking on the very fine Thai bush. He asked what I was up to. I told him I was attempting to learn how to write and confessed he was among my favorite authors. I quickly added Henry Miller and Herman Melville. I told him I'd just read *The Wild Boys* and found it a bit difficult. He said, "*Wild Boys* is not an entirely successful novel. If you read *Port of Saints*, the transition from the Trilogy to *Wild Boys* might be smoother. It's only out in a limited edition. Perhaps I can loan you a copy."

I was a bit shocked at how casually he side-stepped launching a defense of *The Wild Boys*. I had the feeling he knew exactly what I meant and that feeling would become familiar over time...

1978

I finished college and was running a small typesetting business. A friend who was teaching a course on post-WWII American literature at the School of Visual Arts asked me for William Burroughs' phone number so she could arrange a reading. I gave her the info and shortly after William and James Grauerholz appeared at the school, which was just across the street from my digs. It was the first time I'd met James, William's agent and editor, and he was friendly and would prove encouraging, sensing my awe of William. Previously my time with William had been limited to auditing his class at City College, driving him downtown after class in my old VW, and dinners in an assortment of West Village restaurants, but after that reading I found myself invited over often and became a regular at the Bunker.

The Bunker was Burroughs' headquarters at 222 Bowery. It had a large dinner table which came from the conference room of a lawyer's office. Ted Morgan, in his later biography of Burroughs,

Literary Outlaw, would call the regulars at this table "Unconditional Burroughsians." This distinction, appropriate in many ways, discounts the fact that Bill Burroughs did not surround himself with yes-men and discouraged followers. I once ticked him off by agreeing with him so adamantly that he paused the conversation, narrowed his gaze, and asked, "Do you imagine I've got some kind of answers?" What Burroughs thrived on was intelligent opposition. If you found a flaw in one of his theories, you were doing him some good. He was constantly testing his ideas. He possessed a true intellectual distance and would gladly mutate or extend a theme in a new direction after an enlightening discourse. One of the many things William taught me was to assume a "writer's overview" and leave one's ego out of the picture.

The typesetting company had started in a spare room and was now operating two shifts in an office at 72 Fifth Avenue. Alan, my business partner, added a production manager. We had five employees and two steady accounts as well as a growing number of freelance clients. I was group captain on a monthly delivery of eight printer-ready "pulp packages" for Manor Books. It had taken years to build up the business but I could now delegate and pursue my original objective. I wanted to *hang out*. Not like back in Brooklyn, swappin' lies and shootin' the shit. No, I wanted to *hang out* in the European manner: a literary salon, a clique of artists, writers, filmmakers. And as fate would have it that was exactly what was manifesting at the Bunker.

The Bunker was a former industrial loft that had originally served as a locker room. An artist friend of William's, David Prentice, carpentered it into three rooms. Filmmaker Howard Brookner whitewashed the cave-like interior. The largest section featured an alcove kitchen and dining area where the conference table dominated. Across a huge hollow center and facing an inner wall was Burroughs' writing station. An old Bank of England chair sat before a manual Olympia typewriter perched on a big metal office desk. Over the desk hung a Brion Gysin painting titled "Moroccan Street Scene." It looked like an abstract splash of colors until you moved closer and saw the amazingly detailed vision of a cluttered marketplace. The splashes of color were people, their bright clothes mingling. Behind the wall was the archive room, where James Grauerholz lived and maintained the nuts and bolts of Burroughs Communications. Behind James' desk was a dark but roomy closet that contained a skillfully carpentered orgone accumulator built to Burroughs' specifications by David Prentice. The accumulator was invented by Wilhelm Reich as a kind of battery for recharging one's orgones. The third room was Burroughs' bedroom, which contained a bed, a collage screen, a dresser, and another Bank of England chair, which sat in a corner by the sealed industrial window. The thick opaque glass let in a mere modicum of light and was embedded with chicken wire.

If the evening included guests Burroughs

would begin pouring cocktails at six. He leaned on cheap vodka and Coke. Most guests went for tonic with their vodka. His close friend, the poet John Giorno, would come down from his loft upstairs and prep dinner. Burroughs liked to retire early, so if the Bunker was still going strong around nine-thirty or ten and he wished to bow out, he would excuse himself and retire to his bedroom refuge. Often the party would continue for another hour or so and sometimes he would re-appear in a robe on his way to the bathroom.

The bathroom is worth mentioning because it was so typically Burroughsian. The joint had once been a YMCA shower and locker room, so the bathroom was spacious and contained urinals and marble stalls decorated with graffiti. Keith Haring graced one of the stalls with a phallus in simple line work.

The Bunker was an insulated world. You could not hear a thing through the thick walls. You could not tell if it was day or night outside. You could only blind guess the weather. I can still close my eyes and recall the echo of Bill's typewriter banging like thunder.

The Bunker circle in 1978 consisted of a small family of artistic regulars punctuated by visiting luminaries. Whatever guests appeared for dinner were placed among the regulars: James Grauerholz lived in the archive room and proved himself an astute editor of Burroughs' pages and arranger of his daily life. Bill's attachment to James was unbending and together they formed a household. Howard Brookner was a sharp young NYU Film student who was working on a documentary on Burroughs which would win the New York Film Festival award for documentary in 1985. Novelist Steven Lowe had done extensive research on pirate societies. Burroughs was intrigued, as pirates were a key element in a novel-in-progress titled *Cities of the Red Night*. John Giorno was a performance poet and director of Giorno Poetry Systems, which regularly issued spoken word albums featuring Beat and neo-Beat writers. Victor Bockris was a British non-fiction writer, fresh from Andy Warhol's inner Factory circle. Victor had placed numerous interviews and articles on Burroughs in art and literary magazines and was prepping to write a book about the scene we all found ourselves in. Victor also provided a conduit between the Beat and the Punk scenes. Ira Jaffe, a cerebral presence with a wild streak, would later go through NYU Medical and become a surgeon.

Then there were the luminaries: Allen Ginsberg, seminal Beat poet and perhaps the strongest long-standing creative relationship in Burroughs' life. Allen lived a dozen blocks away and was a frequent presence. Ted Morgan, who had recently published a biography of Somerset Maugham and was gathering data for a formal biography of Burroughs. Jeff Goldberg, a crack non-fiction writer who emerged from *High Times* magazine and would soon publish *Flowers in the Blood*, an important early book concerning the discovery of endorphins, the body's production of an opiate-like substance. Herbert Huncke, the aging desperado whose demented fairy tales were being gathered for publication. He was the man who first turned Burroughs on to the magical perils of heroin use. God's Cousin Gregory Corso, who even Allen referred to as an incomparable master of natural poetics. Alan Ansen, who published an early favorable critique of Burroughs and was as astute and literate as a mammal could be. Terry Southern, who wrote *Candy* and *Dr Strangelove*. Publishers John Calder and Maurice Girodias. Rockers Mick Jagger, Lou Reed, Chris Stein, Debbie Harry, Joe Strummer. Artists Keith Haring, David Budd, Andy Warhol, Jean-Michel Basquiat, Brion Gysin. At various times all passed through these chambers. I'm scratching the surface here. The Bunker was a magical context. Imagination was the coin of the realm.

The Bunker salon was strong enough to be a scene even when William was out of town, which was the case through much of 1978, when he found it necessary to spend long stretches of time in Colorado at the Jack Kerouac School of Disembodied Poetics. Allen Ginsberg was the director and had hired him to lecture. Bill was not enthusiastic about teaching in a formal school, but the Kerouac school wasn't nearly as structured as City College. He had lectured there in the past and found the atmosphere agreeable.

The determining factor in his decision to accept the gig was provided by his son Billy, who was in and out of a Boulder hospital making a problematic recovery from a 1976 liver transplant. The new liver had been harvested from the fresh corpse of a Spanish woman named Virginia. Virginia and Billy were engaged in a less than chummy relationship as his body at first rejected the intrusion of a new organ. Things might have settled down in his gut but Billy was fond of beer and morphine.

With Bill in Boulder, James had a lot of free time. My typesetting operation was refined enough to function with minimal supervision, so during the summer of 1978 I spent a lot of time with him. We hung together at the Bunker, took long walks through the Lower East Side, and went out to hear live music. We had dinners with Giorno and dropped in on people we found interesting.

Living with a master stylist had made James into quite a sharp critic and editor. We would talk about writing constantly. One day I told him I was having a problem with my serious writing due to the commercial shit I was forced to produce on deadline. He wisely told me to step back from the serious stuff. His exact words were: "Try to not write and see what emerges." Because of this suggestion, I focused on my daybook. Until that point I had kept no formal journals for years. I had piles of loose notes, consisting mainly of stories, reflections from early life in Brooklyn, conversations I'd had with Burroughs, notes on novels I'd read, ideas, a sentence bank. Burroughs provided a concentrated dip into the challenges facing a writer. I tended to write down whole conversations after seeing him. But these were isolated scraps. Although some were dated these pages were without any attempt at cohesion.

Often we just sat in the Bunker and blew reefers. James was perfect company for a writer because he was open-ended and imaginative. He was deeply worried about Burroughs. James' primary escape from the situation with Billy consisted of kicking back with a guitar. He played a crisp blues guitar with bottleneck slide and remarkably detailed augmentations. He would linger over a bluesy progression as we made up lyrics and goofed. I recall one lyric he dreamed up because it reflected, with humor, a very serious concern. Bill Junior's liver transplant sparked a tribute to the liver's former owner...

>
> Virginia you're my liver
> Though you've got a Spanish soul
> And when you get to pumpin'
> It makes me wanna rock 'n' roll

William's time in Boulder was punctuated by visits to New York for various reasons. The big conference table would fill with the usual faces, and he would hold court with incredibly good humor given what a tough period this was for him. The medical reports on Billy were not promising. The novel William was working on, *Cities of the Red Night*, was not going very strongly, either, despite what ordinarily would be positive factors. He had much of the manuscript and a skillful editor standing by, but Burroughs just could not get to the point where he felt the novel was ready to assemble. This had been going on for some time. It was the tail end of a period of writer's block he'd warned me about.

During this period, I first observed the incredible writer's overview Burroughs was capable of. He had the capacity to be extremely self-confrontational and yet could distance himself from earthly matters when survival or a clear writer's eye depended upon it. From this observation I cultivated an intellectual distance of my own.

One of the most unforgettable lines in the Paris recording, *Call Me Burroughs*, is "For I have known through faulty human equipment the vacant courage to allow all messages in and out." Lyrical and literal, the sentence provides insight into Burroughs' return to Morpheus late in life. I'd speculate that the "vacant courage" is cool. Powdered Cool. Just add water.

In 1978 the Lower East Side was getting a splash and would soon be awash in Powdered Cool: strong cheap heroin. The quality of street dope in Manhattan had substantially weakened in the early seventies. Heat on the Sicilian Mafia resulted in a breaking down of the old supply lines which ran from Turkey, through Italy and France, to Canada or Cuba, and then into the United States. Shit on the street had been weak and expensive. In the late seventies world situations—notably the deposing of the Shah of Iran—brought new product and competition into the circles of street retailing on the Lower East Side, Harlem, Bed-Stuy, and South Bronx. The new ten-dollar bag was smokin'. Due to the Knapp Commission's insights into the cozy relationships between police in the field and large heroin retailing operations, the police were ordered to distance themselves from the street selling scene. The official word was that heroin must be stopped *before* it hits the street. Once it was being retailed, it was to be left alone. Unregulated, crews expanded with the market and began outdoing each other, fighting to present the monster dime bag of the moment. Dealers distinguished their bags with different color tape or a special tuck. The practice of rubber-stamping glassine bags of dope with logos—once a signature of Philadelphia dealers—now provided New York vendadores with the advantage of brand naming. Alphabet City rang with commerce. The corner of Eighth Street and Avenue D ran 24/7 and featured a half-dozen crews competing to be tagged as the smoker of the moment. Open dealing could be observed from Fourteenth Street to Delancey, from Avenue A to the East River. The Toilet Crew huddled around an oil drum fire on Third Street and C. The Green Tape came out of a bodega on Ludlow Street. Demand was high and so was supply. No one had to challenge existing turf. There were plenty of corners, abandoned buildings, and bodegas to deal out of. Word would go out that Dr. Cool was open and smokin'. Next day the jabber would be on Red Line or Black Sunday. Whether or not the people who owned Dr. Nova—which dealt on Rivington Street east of Bowery—were making a literary reference to *Nova Express*, Burroughs got a kick out of their name choice. Schmooz was pouring out of the Puerto Rican social clubs on Eldridge Street just below Houston, off the park benches on Chrystie Street between Rivington and Stanton Streets just a block from the Bunker. And at least a pinch of it was funneling upstairs to the Maestro's door.

William had been clean for over fifteen years. He knew how to play that game and avoided a habit for a while, but the powders were in the air. The art, music, and literary scenes merged with the drug scene: heroin joined cocaine and pot as unavoidable.

Circumstances placed Burroughs in the middle of it all. The Bunker was a living literary salon surrounded by complete dementia. A few blocks uptown at Cooper Square, Third Avenue becomes Bowery and the shift from an artsy, slightly tilted neighborhood to skid row was immediate. Sloshy inebriates danced loose-limbed out of the Bowery's dark taverns to panhandle their next big gulp, falling on the pavement, snoozing in doorways. Junkies wafted off the side streets, navigating in slow-motion through the industrial bustle. Sweat shops, flop houses, warehouses, restaurant supply outlets, dingy loft buildings, curbsides lined with trucks. Street dealing was easy to ignore here. There was so much going on it was just another wrinkle. A near absence of voting citizens and an abundance of flophouse fleas made Bowery perfect for criminal activity. Police prowlers raced around windows up, rarely slowing down let alone stopping. A cop on foot was a rare sight. It seemed the area—like much of the Lower East Side—had been given over to the forces of Chaos. Blending well into the lawless lunacy was CBGB, where the Punk scene burned brightest; ABC No Rio, outside of which the Black Sunday crew held Rivington Street wide open for scoring; and a few druggy art galleries taking advantage of low rents and large raw indoor spaces.

The building at 222 Bowery housed some famous artists as well as the Bunker. It was a pocket of magic situated in dense dystopia. Next door was the Prince Hotel, a flophouse with chicken wire "walls" dividing the sleeping cubicles. Directly across Bowery was the Bowery Mission building. Around the corner was Dr. Nova, keeping patients happy with God's Own Medicine. Through this Burroughsian landscape, the Gray Gentleman would patrol an American version of Interzone on his daily rounds. And anyone visiting would have to navigate through the formation of whiskey-soaked bums that nested on the steps of his evening door.

Dope was available but with it came problems. The limited police presence made scoring easy but dangerous. Armed junkies roamed in search of easy prey and occasionally New York Tactical would step in and bum-rush a spot shotgun first. It could get hairy out there in the field. Getting mugged or arrested was just part of the game.

Even when things went well there were consequences. Strong cheap heroin proves expensive in the long haul. Economics encouraged restraint. Maybe three nights a week we would get high.

Then a timely disaster took place. I had laid some money from my typesetting company on a friend a while back. A minor investment meant only to feed my circle of friends some cheap strong hashish. The friend was a hashish dealer who was between trips. Now he had to leave town. Being an honorable sort, he showed at my door and handed me for collateral a pound of Turkish opium. "In case I can't come back," he explained. I had seen a few grams of O before, but it was an uncommon item in New York City.

Next day I placed half of it in a safety deposit box and brought the other half to the Bunker. I laid it on the big table and watched Bill's eyes glowing with unnatural light. He picked it up and held it like a newborn.

"Now this is something worth gibbering about," he enthused. "We'd better put the kettle on."

I knew little about opium and watched with curiosity as William brewed a pot of tea. He took a sharp blade, heated it, and cut off a few grams. He rolled the pieces in his palms, forming tiny round pills. "I'm not sure of the density so we should weigh these before dropping them. A half gram to a gram should constitute a proper dose."

We adjusted the pills to appropriate weights with a tiny scale. He dropped a full gram with hot and generously sugared tea. I did a half. We sat around the table admiring that big hunk of oily black tar and waiting for the high to kick in.

"Maybe we should smoke a little," I ventured.

"Opium doesn't stay lit by itself," Bill explained. "You need to keep fire on it. A live coal or something. Not a simple matter. Eating it works just fine. Ten or twenty minutes from now you will know all about it."

I remember a strong skeletal relaxation as the high seeped in, a warm equanimity that hit softly without the jolting suddenness of heroin. I just felt good.

What I should have felt was a serious caution because the fat stash of opium marked a fall from the fragile tightrope known as "the chippy." We now had enough shit to fall into the abyss. I left Burroughs with seven one-gram balls. A quarter ounce of pure opium. I pocketed another seven grams. It would be a long time before either of us skipped a few days.

Whatever havoc addiction would later play on his life, the writer in Burroughs was once again active. Bill Burroughs was at his best on the Sacred Substance. The O was working on him like a vitamin complex. The residue of that writer's block he'd been struggling with stepped aside for the Chinaman.

Over the next few months, we got smashed daily but we were both writing. A routine set in. I'd fall by the Bunker mid-morning before going to the office. We'd drop some O and sit around the big table perched over teacups, completely relaxed and absorbed in conversation. Bill would ask me about my Brooklyn amigos. He found their antics amusing. I loved to hear him discourse on books and would try to aim him in the direction of great writing. One morning he went into a long discourse on Graham Greene's novel *A Burnt-Out Case*, concerning a leper who is disfigured but in remission and self-banished to an isolated island leper colony, where his inner life amounted to constant torture. Mesmerized, I only later realized that to William leprosy was a metaphor for the outcaste status of heroin addiction. I was dimly aware of the dangers. You learn to live with these things. I felt magically in control and lacked the experience to identify this blind spot so typical of the early stages of addiction. Besides, my adventures were supplying me with material. I felt lucky and was sure I'd know when it was time to step back. I filled up notebooks feverishly, recording what was happening in the shadows of my life.

When inspiration hit, Bill would get up and waft over to his writing station. Usually I left at this point but sometimes I'd sit there and listen to the rapid bursts of his old manual Olympia typewriter as he leaned into the page.

He addressed the writer in me directly during this period and I learned a great deal. He'd study my pages for a day or two and then let me have it:

"Never follow a great sentence with a mediocre one. The impact of a good sentence should not be broken. Let it end the paragraph or keep that quality going."

"These characters are too similar. They should be clashing, not melting together."

"The trick to dialogue is using your ear. You have your players. Now step back and let 'em talk."

It was blissful to receive his direct attention on my pages, even though almost nothing I produced got the green light. He'd approve a fragment here and there and I'd add it to my bank. I was filling pages and ripping them up at a frantic pace. He saw I was trying. He took my efforts seriously. That was enough for the moment.

At one point a touch of frustration entered my voice and I said, "There's not much more to do with The Word, William. You've burned it down."

But he wasn't buying it. "Look here," he said. "I just scratched the surface. Now you do it."

One evening at dinner he told me and John Giorno about a dream he'd had. "An old Mexican was showing me around a dusty terrain. 'See these roads. These are not unused roads; they are *dead* roads.' The Mexican looked at me as if wondering if the gringo could possibly comprehend such distinctions."

Another evening, at the dinner table, Bill ate the centers out of his lamb chops, pushed the plate away, and reached for the gumdrops. Feeling more than a bit stoned, he broke into his southern preacher routine while chomping noisily. "The Devil is out there inflaming hemorrhoids just to test your faith! Any money you give me goes directly to God!"

Then he did his WASP-from-Hell: "These people don't behave like Amur'cans because they're *not* Amur'cans!"

Giorno and I laughed ourselves purple.

Afternoon tables were a bit more abbreviated. We'd carry on, get high, and laugh our asses off. But at some point, William would get restless, which meant it was time for him to hit the typewriter. I'd go over to the office on Fifth and Fourteenth Street to see how production was going.

Sometimes William would appear at 72 Fifth in the afternoon. His bank was across the street and if he had bank on his list he'd pop by the office for a half hour. I was always pleased to see him in his suit, tan raincoat, and fedora. The office had a cozy private room, and the Bunker faces would fall by often to smoke a bone and shoot the proverbial. My partner, Al, always had some strong exotic leaf to fire up. Al's crew were all into reefer potlatch and very competitive concerning who had the best product, the best sources. If they were around, you could pick up their signature aroma as soon as you walked in.

The office became an extension of the scene. John Giorno would need some typesetting for a new record album. Victor Bockris would sit at one of the keyboards working on his book on Burroughs. James and Howard would flop on the couch and entertain us with goings on in the gay underground. Production took place in the large room facing Fifth Avenue. The small private room seemed a world away.

In a way I'd duplicated the inner sanctum of my boss at the adult fiction factory I'd worked in for six months after graduating from college. That office stank of pot too. If you could make deadlines all sins were forgiven. Soon I'd learned cold-type and in fact the whole process of cheap book preparation: inputting and outputting book pages, correcting errors on a light table, pasting the pages on printer-ready book boards. The printer-publisher demanded eight "literary packages" weekly, which required nasty deadlines, but the writing was mindlessly formulaic—he throbbed; she quivered—and the layout was repetitive: justified margins 12 picas across, 16 picas down, central pagination.

I got this job from an ad in the *Village Voice* for "Adult Fiction Writers." You had to produce 188 output pages weekly: 125 single-spaced typewriter pages. William found this amusing. I reminded him that when we first met at City College in 1974, he suggested I fill a ream of paper and throw it away just to warm up. That job served the same purpose. I learned typesetting and basic cold-type book production and I learned to sit at the keyboard whether I felt like it or not. By the late 1970s I owned half of a typesetting business, and it allowed me the time and cash to follow my calling.

Near the end of 1978, a playful Frenchman named Sylvère Lotringer appeared at the Bunker with a vision. "I wish to create a series of events that will celebrate William Burroughs in a way that will make waves in the media," he announced.

Sylvère was a Columbia professor and the publisher of *Semiotext(e)*. He had a profile on and off campus. He wished to plan and execute a series of events called "The Nova Convention" as an homage to Burroughs' work and influence on other artists, writers, and musicians. James and John jumped on the vision and a campaign was born. It would take considerable time to develop but plans began and would become increasingly elaborate as the end of the 1970s approached.

The idea was a natural. Burroughs was down for doing readings. He had been coached by James and now liked putting on a show. An international following was flowering. He was receiving some recognition from the academics lately and was widely regarded as an inspiration in the Punk world. The up-and-coming literary and music scenes were rich with stylistic and sometimes direct references to Burroughs' writings. Several famous rock 'n' rollers were fans and maybe a few would perform to beef up the draw. Patti Smith and Frank Zappa agreed. Keith Richards sent promising signals but finally backed out. The B-52s found their way into the pudding.

My role in the Nova Convention was modest but rewarding. I hired a passenger van and drove Burroughs and a small circle of close friends from gig to gig. The van's interior would invariably fill with pot smoke and goofy conversations as the Burroughs Mob ferried from reading to party and back to the Bunker. This went on for a good number of weeks.

The highlight for me was spending travel and hang-out time with Terry Southern, who proved to be an entertaining presence. He was particularly enlightening when it came to women.

"Stew, you've got a problem with that blonde demolition expert," he counseled, referring to a willowy blonde named Leslie, a bright young art student who absolutely had me by the horns. "I suggest a bathtub filled with wet teenyboppers as an immediate cure. Or if you'd rather drag it out, electric shock administered thrice a day during the prime masturbation hours."

Painter and writer Brion Gysin often sat beside me in the front seat. I never quite hit it off with Gysin, who eyeballed me with more suspicion than curiosity. This might have been my fault. I'd heard William speak of him so often I felt as if we were acquainted and so I was a touch too relaxed around him. A little visible esteem was in order. The man who defended the lack of linear narrative structure in *Naked Lunch* by identifying the book's relationship to the "collage technique used by painters" had a rather elitest personal style. I was a friend of William's so he was polite, but I'm sure he dismissed me as a street kid. I wasn't gay, wasn't yet published, and did not look at him with open awe. There was no opening for chumminess. I did admire his paintings and perhaps should have said so.

The first winds of Nova blew for a few months, as events were added. Dope and reefers around the big table. Familiar faces laughing into the night.

Howard Brookner would spend hours in the archive room with piles of footage trying to edit the documentary that he was making on Burroughs. His eyes would roll from the effort. He and his NYU film crew were efficient and sharp and had filmed an amazing volume that was still building. One afternoon he showed me a half hour of Allen Ginsberg chanting with his harmonium.

"The outtakes are going to be as interesting as what remains in the film," I ventured.

Howard moaned. "Outtakes? There's still shooting to do! Will there ever be an end to this?"

1978

SATURDAY, JANUARY 28ᵀᴴ, 1979
Sitting at the Bunker with Giorno. William still out of town. We're talking about William's cut-up trilogy: *The Soft Machine*, *Nova Express*, and *The Ticket That Exploded*.

"Bill's *Cities* represents a dramatic evolution in his writing style," I said. "That worries me a bit. I think those early novels are fantastic."

"Yes," John agreed. "But William's always moving on. I don't know what's on his mind, but a great writer has to stay in motion." He told me Bill was a bit uptight during his recent two weeks in New York. He would be back in the summer.

SUMMER 1979
Howard saw the Burroughs documentary as a means of preserving the animated greatness of an important American writer. Burroughs was getting older and while his work would live,

the man himself would one day join the general humidity.

At the time there was a rich pool of great writers pushing the years out there. Alex Trocchi, Jean Genet, Samuel Beckett, Tennessee Williams. One of my favorite old cooties was James T. Farrell. I opened the *New York Times* one day in August of 1979 and received a depressing bit of news. Farrell had checked out. The Studs Lonigan trilogy, as shocking in its day as *Huck Finn*, constituted a modern manifestation of "social realism." I'd returned to it a dozen times over the years. Farrell knew how to tell a story. I'd been handed Studs as a kid and related easily: first to the urban setting and later to the visible mixture of unhappiness and hope that filled the characters. In the beginning Studs has that strut, that arrogance of youth. Anything's possible. As he grows the rich lantern of potential starts to flicker. Maybe nothing will happen. He's incorporated into his father's house-painting business. The Depression is coming, and work slows down. The love of his life dumps his ass. The social order, once rich with promise, turns against him and he has no real comprehension of how it happened or what to do about it. The enemy is carefully hidden, so he blames those in front of him. The Jews. The blacks. Meanwhile blacks are moving into his nabe. His sister marries a prosperous young Jewish bookie. He knocks up a girl he has only a faint affection for and must marry and support her. In the end he's out in the rain looking for work to support this unwelcome but inevitable household, gets a cold, and croaks. Not with a bang but with a whimper.

One night in the Bunker I asked William what he thought of Farrell's most interesting novel. He said, "That Marxist Socialist element never appealed to me, but the man told a good story and caught that period. Chicago. Dark clouds over post-WW I prosperity. The Depression. Union organizers whispering in the shadows. Scabs. Picket lines. Soup lines."

"The unions were a good thing, hey?"

"At first. Like the Mob they became little more than a branch of government. But Farrell caught much of what was wrong with the country at a given time. That alone has a value. Making the novel into a trilogy causes a bit more bulk than is necessary."

"Sometimes substance takes space," I defended.

"Man, even space takes space. One of the best-plotted novels in the English language is *Dr. Jekyll and Mr. Hyde* and it's maybe a hundred pages. Splendid writing. The chill is there but you can't quite point to it. You have educated evil looking to burst free. The good Doctor is getting curious. What lurks beneath my mannered exterior? So he mixes up a concoction designed to invoke his dark side. He drinks this bubbling goo and wham! Pure evil! Don't look in the mirror. But hell, that was fun. Let's do it again. A few more doses and the transformation takes place spontaneously. No need for the potion. The dark side's gaining ground, getting stronger. Just the thought of it paints a leer of lust and venom on the Doctor's face. Tasty! Perfect metaphor."

"Metaphor for what?"

"For what? Come on man! The magician summons an abomination. The Beast appears but he's angry. You disturbed his slumber. The Beast is obliged to perform but now there's a problem. He wants a sacrifice. Maybe the magician himself. Who has got the weight in this situation?"

"Ol' Doc got in a little deep, hey?"

"Well, he should have prepared for the inevitable. Did he know a spell of containment? Of banishment? See man, he was not ready for the consequences of his magic."

"But when you speculate you're always out on a limb."

"Okay, sure, but there is a price, that's all. You want to write a great book or create a great painting; you might have to first take yourself over the edge. But as a writer, as an artist, your primary responsibility is to come back and do the work."

One day the hashish dealer sent an associate of his to pay me off and reclaim the remaining O. I had very little gummy goodness left, so the guy stuffed the envelope of money back in his inner jacket pocket and gave me a look. He was not surprised.

Sitting around the Bunker with Bill one night we began to talk about Buddhism. This occurred because Giorno's guru was in town, and we were watching him sprint around making himself useful.

"The idea of karma has a certain appeal," I ventured. "But there's a downside. You pass a slum-bum begging on the street. The Judeo-Christian concept of charity would be to give the guy a smoke and two bucks or at the very least feel bad about passing him by. The karma thing, it seems, would be hey, fuck the sucker. The cat's doin' a skid bit for some bad shit he laid out in a previous lifetime."

Bill said that he had no interest in defending karma or Buddhism for that matter but remarked that "John is a good student who has picked up the best qualities of the old man." He went on: "John has an amazingly apparent sense of integrity in these matters and whether or not you take Buddhism seriously you have to take John's relationship to it seriously."

Then we spoke about some pages I'd handed William a week ago. I'd stopped mid-story and he asked me why.

"Something was starting to emerge," he said. "Why didn't you develop it?"

"I'm sitting there writing and everything's fine. Then I start watching myself and start to lose it."

William was silent for a moment, then asked, "Who's watching you when you're watching yourself? And just *who* is being watched?"

WEDNESDAY, JULY 4ᵀᴴ, 1979

Fireworks. Always amazed me that combat vets or in fact anyone who's ever been shot at could enjoy loud rapid-fire explosions. The Lower East Side went bonkers. Hells Angels closed off East Third Street and were detonating atomic weapons under an American flag that was huge enough to hang over and dominate the street. The Death's Head symbol and Old Glory flickered in the explosions. Roman candles and skyrockets sailed through the darkening skies over the East River.

On my usual walk from the apartment on East 21ˢᵗ Street east of Third Avenue to the Bunker on Bowery and Prince Street, I encountered a huge crowd spilling out of CBGB and most of them were higher than I was. They were lighting firecrackers, drinking, and smoking reefers, their eyes glassy and wild. Junkies drooled. Juicers guzzled. Speedballers jabbered. A mist of lush sweat, puke, and stale beer permeated the air. Often the scheduled bands would keep people waiting for hours while they were waiting for their heroin to arrive.

It was an amazing time to be in New York City. Persian White pouring in since the Shah of Iran got bounced. The old French White was back on the scene. The Cuban Chinese cliques—fortunate enough to speak Spanish and Chinese—running their powders through New York's Barrio Chena. Some Burmese White coming in through smuggling lines left over from Vietnam. Even the old standard Mexican brown could be found if one tripped over to Sunset Park or Bushwick.

All these street crews competed for the New York City market. Dime bags that kicked ass made a comeback. I got chummy with Kono, the Puerto Rican cat who bossed the Black Sunday crew. He had a taste for good reefer, and I'd throw him a bud now and again just to hang and shoot the shit. Of course he'd reciprocate, slipping me a few bags of dope.

I was fascinated by the language these crews employed. How they acted and communicated in the field was intriguing. Words were cooked down to the essentials. Their communication was abbreviated, musical, and organic: a whistle followed by a gesture or a few words in Spanish called out from a tenement roof. If one of the peeps cried "Fao!" everything stopped, and the crew just dissolved into air. I asked Kono what "fao" meant and he told me: "ugly." It was their word for plainclothes cops. Every few hours the boss would take a walk to drop off bank and pick up material. Ten grand per stroll. And he'd take this walk four or five times a day. That was one spot. Black Sunday also had crews in the Bronx and in Williamsburg. "Where the fuck is all that money going?" I wondered. Day after day, brown paper bags stuffed with cash!

The local precinct cops were barely present and hardly disruptive. Manhattan South kicked ass but were rarely on-set. When they were, they aimed at low-level workers. They'd haul off a few scramblers and knock out a spot for an hour or two. The remaining workers would open two blocks away and finish their packages. The crews adapted instantly to police moves. Rooftop lookouts signaled the touters, who stood on specific corners and told customers where to find the scramblers. Field operations were layered and compartmentalized to avoid police penetration. You gave cash to one worker and picked up from another. The Red Line crew on East Third Street west of Avenue D worked an abandoned building in a way no one saw who was selling. A familiar face would nod you in. Then a bucket would come down through a hole in the ceiling of one of the apartments. Drop your cash in the bucket and up it goes. Then back down with your bags. The Dr. Nova crew working out of Seven Rivington Street was the most consistent. You'd turn the corner off Bowery. If the dark-skinned cholo with the newsboy cap was sitting on a crate outside of 7 Riv, they were open. You walked in and waited in line in a long corridor. If the cops came, the peep outside would shut the door and the crew just disappeared, leaving a half dozen confused junkies awaiting their fate. I was very lucky on the street, even when I took the dumbest chances. It's potluck. The joker in the car behind you gets dogged, but you're alright. Question is: how alright are you? It's just a matter of time...

  There were three crews working within a block of William's digs. The shift from Bowery chaos to the Bunker involved only the most abbreviated transition. Open the iron gate, climb a flight of stairs, and bingo. Quietude. Maybe a little Bach or Billie Holiday playing but more likely a supreme silence. Thick walls of an industrial building.

Books all around. Teacups on the table.

Later that night at the big table William made a Fourth of July toast. "I'd like to take this moment to thank ol' Daddy George for the utterly bestial strategy of attacking on God's birthday."

He went into a routine about the American Revolution. "All of five thousand people fought in the Revolution. As wars go it was doodle-squat, but with a very real sincerity to it. A valid idealism. A gentleman's game. Nowadays war is just an excuse to depopulate terrain for monied interests."

SATURDAY, SEPTEMBER 1ST, 1979

I'd been re-reading some old shit, notably *Oliver Twist*. Ol' Fagin was so familiar I felt like we did some whispering together in another life and maybe had a falling out but some mutual sympathy remained. Rowdy familiars crowded around the Old Bones as he sits at the piano tinkling out maybe the only smile these little perverts have ever worn.

Sitting at the big table one afternoon being peeped coldly by Doctor Benway I took a shot. "What do you think of Fagin, William? I think he was some kind of hero."

"What?" His neck jerked up in response. "Are you crazy?"

His eyes only opened that wide when he was appalled by my stupidity. I felt some shaky ground coming but went on. "Look, these street urchins are stealing silk hankies from overfed overbred shitbags who'd happily stomp over their corpses if they died on the street. There are no social services going on. This is desperation... survival."

"Now you are saying that the effect of your actions can be positive even though your intentions were evil. Sure, the opposite is also a possibility. You can fuck everything up with the best intentions. Aristotle was trying to clear the mud with his either/or thinking. What he did was sidestep the dialectic. I'm sure the ancient Hebrews were only trying to make life easier with their One God approach to cosmology. What they did was open the door to cosmic monopoly. Cause-and-effect is unspecific at the bottom line. But let's stick to the author's intentions—"

"Which might've been hidden—"

"Stew, it's like you're making a hero out of Iago."[*]

William's tone called for an immediate change of subject. We moved on to one of his favorites and soon he was in a dreamy reminiscence about the sterling strength of three-dollar papers of quinine-kissed Goodness on 103rd Street and Broadway in the mid-to-late forties.

"Just a bit after the War this shit started trickling into New York. There'd been a terrible shortage you know. The first few people to hit New York with good material must have cleaned up. Anyway, this particular score uptown... you

---

[*] A year or so later I brought this idea to Jacques Stern, who almost screamed, "Fagin is the manifestation of survival!"

could scratch grooves in your cheeks from that quinine but maaan did that schmeck pack a flash."

SUNDAY, SEPTEMBER 2ND, 1979
Next day I marched into the Bunker with Dom, one of my berserker runnin' buddies from the wild and woolly days. Dom had come a long way since we were kids in Brooklyn. He'd earned some favor with the Dark Gods and was privy to a direct line of uncut heroin from Pleasant Avenue, but he recalled the lean years and loved hearing old scoring yarns. I knew Bill had a million of them and felt like taking a chance and bringing him to the Bunker one night. On the way over Dom asked what drew me to William Burroughs. I said, "First time I read him I realized: This is a master writer and a highly evolved criminal mind." Dom smiled. He understood.

We entered the Bunker. I introduced them. Firm handshakes, easy smiles. By the time we sat down at the big table I could see they were curious about each other.

"Specs tells me you used to score on Upper Broadway in the 1940s," Dom opened. "What was that like?"

"There was no open dealing. You had to know the faces and if you knew them the cops knew them. Many's the time I couldn't score and had to hit a doctor for a script."

Don smiled in sympathy. "Drag yer sick ass to the doctor. Times have changed, hey? Dope all over the Lower East Side. How's the quality these days?"

"A lot better than the old days. Puerto Rican crews competing with the Dominicans for smoker of the day."

"Yeah, that's what I'm hearing. Anyway, I'm not the most literary guy around so I brought along something to lubricate conversation." Dom flipped a thumb over a nostril and whipped out a golf ball size chunk of God's Own. "That's kilo-quality Number 4 white," he said, placing it on the table. "Chipped right off the block, not reconstituted. It's the real thing. Caution is in order."

"Oh!" Bill's eyes popped open. He rubbed his hands together.

Doctor Benway began to emerge before our eyes. "Where is my cooker?" he asked.

They were both priming their weepers and prepping their cookers. Dom shaved off a solid half gram and crushed it with the handle of a knife. He used the blade to place a bit of powder on a small mirror and put it before me. I sniffed a small line of it through a rolled-up dollar bill. I never used needles. Didn't like the blood and was never big on the flash. The opium—my first habit—gave me a taste for that slow creeping-up contentment. Sniffing or smoking did the trick. I broke open a Thai stick to roll a joint, into which I sprinkled a dusting of the Number 4. We were kicking back, relaxing, all was well. The Doc and his guest were untying their arms. Their gimmicks sat on a piece of newspaper Bill had placed on the table.

Doc cracked the silence: "So Dominick, how's life in the Mafia?"

I almost shit my jeans. You don't use words like that around guys like Dom. Protocol would be for him to issue a dirty look, get up, and storm out of the room upon hearing that word, but he just smiled and said, "There is no Mafia, Mr. Burroughs. It's a rumor spread by people who don't like Italians."

"Hmff! Hmff! Hmfff! Of course. God, what was I thinking?"

"Even J. Edgar Hoover knew that," Dom added.

"And who would doubt such a noble man. Bit of a blackmailer of course. Capable of vast assaults on human dignity. Well, I'm sure he had his good points."

As the high descended things got a little rubbery. Time might have passed. Hard to tell.

"This is some fine shit," William decided.

"Um hm."

I don't recall lighting the infused joint but there it was between my fingers smoking away. I took a hit and was immediately sorry. I tried passing it to Dom. I considered a stroll to the vomitorium.

"Get away from me with that shit," Dom said.

"Put that out," William added.

The playful sociability in the room had faded. We were all on the brink of nodding out. Dom had anticipated this and reached in his pocket for the energizer. We each did a line of cocaine. Now properly speedballing, Doctor Benway took on the role of a high-toned career counselor and advised me to write a great novel so that I could refer to my drug indulgences as "meritorious research."

Before we split Dom chipped a few grams off the white rock to leave for his distinguished new friend.

Burroughs had an impressive tolerance for Dom, who was great fun but could go a little beyond the confines of sanity. They only met once more before Dom disappeared. One evening William did a reading at the Mud Club, with Giorno opening for him. I fell by with Dom and my partner in the typesetting business. Dom quickly situated himself at the pool table and sparked a game of crazy eights. When the reading ended William, Dom, Al, and I ran through a driving rain and piled into Dom's goosed-up Mustang. Bill and I got in the back. Al sat next to Dom in the front. I saw Dom slide a semi-automatic under his seat, light a joint, and peel out like a crazed teenager. Rain-slicked streets made the rear end slide out every time he popped the clutch. After a few blocks he curbed, then pulled out a tray and some powder. We each did a fat line and hit the road again, back to roastin' rubber and weaving around saner drivers.

"Slow down, Dom," Al let out. "You're gonna get us pinched."

Dom smiled. "Relax. I was born lucky."

After a screeching left turn threw me against William and pressed us both to the side window,

I also got on Dom's case. "If we get popped with Bill in the car it's gonna be a headline bust. Slow this pony down."

"What's with this limp-dick shit! Bill don't look worried."

He was right about that. William was laughing. Unfortunately, his amusement triggered Dom to new heights of lunacy.

Vroooom!

"William. You're encouraging him. If you laugh he'll just keep it up!"

William tried to look serious—even stern for a second—but he burst out laughing again.

"If you get us collared I'm gonna rip your face off," Al spit. "This is baby shit."

Dom shrugged and nailed the gas, roasting rubber into a driving rain. Chrystie Street has a pedestrian break through the narrow strip of Roosevelt Park at Stanton Street. You are not supposed to drive through it, but Dom promptly did. We hit the curb with a thump, jumped it, and flew through to the other side.

"You're fuckin' crazy!" Al bellowed.

"Hey Dom, you're pushing this shit," I added.

William was laughing his ass off at this point. Something in him was enjoying our terror and Dom's teasing. When we finally curbed on Bowery near the Bunker, Dom sought refuge walking next to William, the only one not pissed at him.

William asked about Dom a few times over the next year. I repeated what I'd been told, which was that he had heavy warrants out for him, got some fresh ID papers, and booked it out of New York. This was pre-computer days and shit like that could play forever. William took in the information and did not look surprised.

As the 1970s moved along, my life was frantic yet oddly in order. I had a typesetting business going two shifts. I was in the company of Bill Burroughs and his associates on a daily basis. I was gathering material as a writer. On the negative side, the marriage I'd entered at age twenty was falling apart and I had a dope habit. I was engaged in little side-adventures that could have landed my ass in the zoo at any time. My reasoning was that anyone making money beyond a salary—in the mainstream or in the shadows—was constantly waiting to be indicted. Like most of my thinking at the time, something was missing. Namely, a solid foot on the ground.

Writing requires daydreaming, which requires a budget. What I needed was time. What I got was a blur of activity.

Somehow, I was balancing endless details among my partner, our typesetters, and assorted art directors and production managers from our typesetting accounts. But the procedures had been established and unless there was a shit-fit, pressure was containable. Crinkles only happened when a deadline was approaching and something went wrong: a machine problem or a font we didn't have in-house and couldn't locate. In situations like that I'd get on the horn and throw a foaming fit.

If the Bunker scene was taking a turn towards Chaos, it was only a prelude of things to come. A major modulation developed when James decided to move back to Lawrence, Kansas, where he had gone to college. He would handle William's business affairs from this small river town in the Midwest, where life was slow and inexpensive. James had enormous editing responsibilities and New York City was not a relaxing place to tear through William's raw copy, arrange readings, and deal with publishers. Also, James could not bring himself to approve of William's heroin use. It was great that Bill was writing again but using dope was dangerous and expensive. At any rate, James' relocation proved to be a good move as William would eventually join him in Lawrence and find himself set up with a cozy scene in which to write and paint. But the immediate impact of his move was that Bill was on his own in drug-drenched late-seventies Lower Manhattan.

With James out of New York, William could live his life free of paperwork and other earthly complications. He enjoyed entertaining interesting people at the big table in the evenings. Bill was not the kind of guy to get on the horn and spark this kind of thing. Someone else had to do it and so Victor Bockris contributed to William's intellectual stimulation by arranging dinners at the Bunker.

Bockris' enthusiasm for William was boundless and resulted in many memorably guested dinner gatherings. Some were problematic, some were smashingly successful, and all of them were interesting. These events are well covered in his book, *With William Burroughs: A Report from the Bunker*. The Christopher Isherwood dinner was an exercise in good manners and literary camaraderie. Mick Jagger falls under problematic but stormy and stimulating. A dinner with Debbie Harry and Chris Stein led to a lifelong friendship. Andy Warhol's presence produced a shimmering banality that lingered in the Bunker for days.

I once asked William why Warhol carried himself with such breathlessly bland excitement. He replied, "It's his prosaic charm, my dear. The pose of a fourteen-year-old girl leaping from petulant to bubbly. Interviewer asks, 'Where do you think the art world is going, Mr. Warhol?' After what might or might not be a thoughtful pause Andy looks at his nails, says, 'Ahh, anybody got any gum?'"

MONDAY, SEPTEMBER 3RD, 1979

Labor Day at the Bunker.

I asked Bill, "Is a tightrope walker a tightrope walker all the time?"

"What do you mean?"

"I mean that's a highly focused activity. It's bound to lock one in."

"Oh I see. Like dancers. That's all they talk about. Now a tightrope walker is very specialized. When you advance in one area you tend to filter everything you see and hear through the criteria of that area. The idea of being intensely specific must take on a significant meaning. He can be other things perhaps, but he'd better not forget he's a tightrope walker. The last thing he'd want is to do is think about it while he's up on the high wire. Maybe some pre-thinking. Factors of the trade. Is there a strong wind? Is it steady or sporadic? Maybe you can lean into a steady wind, but it better hold steady and you'd better be ready if it doesn't. As for myself, I will continue to cower in the Bunker and leave that shit to the professionals."

I was half asleep on the office couch one afternoon when a call came in. One of our typesetters was stranded in a very understanding Puerto Rican lady's crib on East Third Street near Avenue D. He'd been mugged while scoring dope in the hallway of her building. The creeps took his dope and his Bermuda shorts so he couldn't follow them. He knocked on the lady's door and begged to use her phone, explaining the situation.

Frankly I was a bit pissed. Who in their right mind goes marching into Alphabet City wearing Bermuda shorts? But he was a good typesetter and was working on a project with a strict deadline. Instead of worrying about my problems, I was worrying about his. I dispatched another typesetter to buy the cheapest, loudest pants available at a discount store on 14th Street and bring them to this unfortunate shitbag, who was now causing two typesetting stations to be empty. "Try to find a nice bright purple or banana yellow.

Maybe with a target over the ass," I suggested. "And make sure they're very large."

"Oh, you love him, don't you!" Rosie jubilated. She was a decent typesetter. A very pretty girl but a shameless and dedicated flatulent, an arena in which she earned status as an exhibitionist.

New Year's Eve 1980 was still a few months off but John Giorno was planning a large party and I had a decision to make. He'd invited Allen Ginsberg, Peter Orlovsky, Lucien Carr, and Herbert Huncke and his sidekick Louis Cartwright, as well as the expanded cliques that had formed around the Beat writers over the years. Who would I invite, April or Leslie?

I was still married to April even though we rarely spent time together. She possessed an academic brilliance and was now an editor at Schirmer Books. The title gave her a substantial platform for imposing her opinions as hard law. If you disagreed with her on a literary matter, she would quickly pull rank. I decided to pass on inviting her to a party full of old Beat writers and their circles because she was more at home with editors than writers. Writers are unpredictable and push the strictures of correct behavior. They are children. They are annoying and self-indulgent.

As for Leslie, I was crazy about her but the relationship had evolved into a strong mixture of reverie and frustration. She was creative, impossibly beautiful, and demanding. Banging her was unearthly and sweet but generally she was a major distraction, doling out affirmation in small installments designed to keep me fired-up and guessing. She'd been modeling for a year or so and had recently dominated the cover of the Paris *Vogue*, which just made her more difficult and erratic. She wanted to go to this party and called me regularly to sniff it out.

After much chemical contemplation I decided to go alone. That way I could hang with Bill, relax, and check out the people.

MONDAY SEPTEMBER 10TH, 1979

The office shit was driving me to distraction. Manor Books was cooling the sex line for a few months and switched me over to McFadden Romances. This deal required four literary packages a month instead of eight with the erotic stuff, but it was harder to find writers for this material. It was not just wall-to-wall biology. There had to be an actual plot, continuity, some sort of story. Nothing challenging of course. Just the usual: the brooding hero and moist maiden. He's tortured by some dark secret and barks at her or slaps her. She falls in love with him. The crescendo builds with her pain and peaks when he pukes out his secret: he has been hurt in the past. Boo fuckin' hoo. But now he loves her. A few punishing kisses and fade...

As annoying as it is to pump out pulp bullshit, this is a matter of staying afloat. We've lost a few accounts due to IBM's new equipment, which includes the Selectric Composer's capacity to output justified copy with proportional spacing. This cuts into our position in the marketplace. Some publishers—notably *Playboy*'s paperback line—are not all that quality-conscious and have taken their production in-house. We lose another account to the situation and figure there's more bad news down the road. My group caption slot with Manor Books—which switches from month to month between romance novels and erotica—is a fucking nightmare I'd love to dump but is now completely essential. Easy enough to hire people to pump out erotica but the romances are harder. People write a few then drop out, leaving me to write them.

I switched to a Dictaphone for this assignment. Three ninety-minute cassettes filled a book. One of our typesetters was accustomed to working from tapes and took over the keyboarding. Still, I had to mutter this dreadful shit into a microphone and it became more distasteful with every cassette I filled. Just maintaining continuity was an effort. What was that character's name again? Where the fuck was this story taking place?

My cousin Alice, fresh out of college, took it upon herself to write one. A few other writers stepped up and managed a book or two. No one seemed to be able to produce more than one a month. To maintain my position as group captain I had to wallow in this shit.

I spoke to William on the phone and thanked him for the blackjack he'd given me the previous night at the Bunker. We'd broken open a few glassine bags of Dr. Nova, which I'd scored earlier. Much stronger than most street dope. I asked him if he'd seen the group of poems Giorno had my staff typeset. Bill laughed and said, "His Dalai Lama is in town. John's running around like a chicken with his head chopped off, arranging dinners and events, meetings with people the Dalai Lama would like to meet, or John feels would be useful or of interest to his teacher."

"That's dedication."

I envied John's ability to focus on what was important to him. I did not always have that luxury. I'd always found it depressing when the schmutz work began taking precious orgones away from serious writing. As usual I had little choice. This was one of the patterns of my life. Money pressures overriding creative efforts. On the flip side, the need to make bucks was what got me out into the world. The barking hounds of commerce were feeding me important elements that would one day show up on my pages. But those same canines were whittling away my energy.

Everything was fine and everything was fucked-up. I paid off this credit card but that one was nailing me. We made our payroll but the corporate taxes cooked our bank account.

WEDNESDAY SEPTEMBER 12TH, 1979

Leslie showed up at the office looking tempting as ever, so I sent the two typesetters home for the night. We dropped opium and fell into a dreamy sensual suspension of time culminating in deep sleep unbroken until morning brought the dayshift.

THURSDAY SEPTEMBER 20TH, 1979

Didn't see William yesterday. Spoke on the phone about Graham Greene, Conrad, *Apocalypse Now*. When I got to the office today, I found him sitting on the couch reading and poking on a Thai Stick joint. I told him I'd skipped a few days in the past month just to see what would happen and was not very uncomfortable. A little hashish took my mind off heroin. Bill warned me about losing my fear of schmooz. He assured me that there is a line that once crossed would produce a much more dramatic impact upon which a little hashish would have no relief.

Later that day, the phone rang and Burroughs asked me to answer it. "If it's Jacques Stern again, tell him I'm not here."

It wasn't Jacques Stern, but my curiosity was bursting. I'd heard of the infamous Jacques before. He had been a serious influence on Burroughs during the Beat Hotel years in Paris, as *Naked Lunch* was being written. In fact, William had acknowledged in a letter to Allen Ginsberg dated September 25, 1959, that "The end of *Naked Lunch* is addressed to Jack, as he must know." (Bill often referred to Jacques by the Americanized "Jack.") He went on to say, "I learned more from Jack than from anyone else I ever knew, except Brion."

"Is there a problem here?" I asked.

"No, not really. The Baron and I go way back. Sometimes I just can't deal with him. He's in a wheelchair. Densely intellectual. A rich French aristocrat. The man runs hot and cold. Lately he's been stormy and unbearable. Jacques at his best is brilliant, inspiring. His background includes physics, math, anthropology. He speaks dozens of languages and just bubbles with ideas and concepts and can take any thought you have directly where it's going, complete with inferences, alternates, variables, surprise endings."

"Sounds smashing."

"A great presence while you're writing. That's when he's on. At his worst, he can try the patience of a corpse."

"Was he somehow involved in the project to film *Junkie*? I think Howard mentioned that name once or twice."

"Yes, yes he was. The Baron initiated that plan and infused it with cash. Troops were called in. Terry Southern to do the script writing. Dennis Hopper to play the ever-degraded William Lee. Jacques had his twenty-three-year-old wonder boy, Joe Bianco, handling the cash flow."

"Why was no film made?"

William smiled. "It was more an exercise in madness than a film project. Jacques had these swanky digs on Gramercy Park where he threw promotional parties. He put Dennis and Terry up in the Gramercy Park Hotel so they were close at hand and easy to torment. Booze, speed, and cocaine had everybody all lovey-dovey one minute and at war the next. Jacques offered no stability to the atmosphere. A hyper guy in an electric wheelchair, always buzzing around. It would not be incomprehensible to imagine that Terry modeled the Peter Sellers character in the wheelchair in *Doctor Strangelove* on Jacques. 'Doomsday' was Jacques' mantra. A brilliant guy but always instigating. Little beefs turn into big balloons of anger. He's got Hopper barking at him. Now he's barking at Terry. I tried to keep out of it. Now they're both on separate phones barking at others. James took most of the brunt."

"Jacques was tough on James?"

"Well, James and Joe Bianco, they were sort of the adults. I don't think either of them had turned twenty-four, so not in years, but in temperament. Bianco was one of those young financial warriors who just breathes money into situations. Very astute business mind. Investors following him around and breathing down his neck. Yale Law School. Didn't drink or get high. Both feet on the ground. And James of course remained reasonable and articulate even through the worst of it. The funding died. We were all very disappointed. Jacques lost his investment, which was considerable. This happened during the period when you were just out of college and starting your business, Stew. You missed the performance."

"I'm hearing it now. What's the current on

Jacques Stern?"

William shrugged. "Just emerging from one of his darker periods. This happens when his very wealthy French family gets ticked off. He gets a phone call from Paris instead of a check in the mail. The party is over until he straightens out. No male nurse shooting him full of coke or speed. No cushion under his ass. He's very stubborn and will not tell them what they want to hear. It can go on for months. During these periods he can be a living menace."

"How much mischief can a guy in a wheelchair get into?"

William laughed. "Stew, you can only imagine. Anyway, I've been speaking to him when he calls. I helped him out a few times. He even spent a week in the Bunker a while back when he got tossed out of the Chelsea Hotel. It was useless. I couldn't have him around and live my life. He completely breaks my work pattern."

"Kicked out of the Chelsea? What a distinction. Joint's full of junkies and jokers."

"Jacques and Harry Smith both lived in the Chelsea. They were at war. What Doctor Graves once called 'The War of the Wizards.' Jacques was paying Harry's rent, which only pissed Harry off. The damage was extensive and endless."

"Gee, kicked out of the Chelsea..."

"The Baron is a man of complexities and was a great help to me while I was writing *Naked Lunch*. Portions of the text were directly influenced by him. This was noted in the first

Olympia Press edition published in Paris in 1959. Jacques' name was omitted from further editions at his insistence. He was a true recluse and wanted no attention. An expanded version of human intellect. A sly imagination. Rolling his wheelchair through a vast private library, with nothing to do but suck up those books." Burroughs looked at me. "He's often acted in the role of patron to writers he considers promising. During the Beat Hotel period, he'd save my ass now and again. Showing up with much-needed heroin, throwing a few bucks my way, taking our little group out to dinner. In fact, the *Junkie* film project was initiated with checks for twenty thousand bucks each laid on me, Terry Southern, and Dennis Hopper. Got me over a tight spot. One day we will have pages of yours to show him."

"Sounds like a very mixed blessing."

"Most blessings are. But this one's worth it. He's in possession of a very penetrating intelligence and a form of enlightenment. The wheelchair is necessary because his legs are withered from an early bout with polio. Yet he exhibits a distance from these conditions. It's as if he doesn't take his limitations, or for that matter the physical universe, all that seriously. Mere terrestrial matters."

"That is impressive."

"That says a lot about a man's spirit."

FRIDAY SEPTEMBER 21ST, 1979

On the phone with William.

Bill: I read your piece. A few stray ends and displacements but you're moving your characters along.

Me: I know what I want to catch. I want my characters breathing. You're in the room with 'em.

Bill: Your characters are vivid but something's off. Only you can figure out what. Experiment freely. Walk around with them. What do they want? Will they go beyond fear to get it?

On my way to see William I thought about Downtown Manhattan as a detached context, alive with art and chaos. Many of the people who had inspired the new aesthetics were still around and visible: Allen Ginsberg, Andy Warhol, Bob Dylan, William S. Burroughs. Galleries were opening all over the Lower East Side. Art, literature, music, and dope scenes melted together. Readings at St. Mark's. Music pouring out of CBGB. You could go catch Ray "Sugar" Hernandez, Patti Smith, Blondie, the Ramones, or the hellacious and spectacular saxophone sounds of James Chance. These people lived sporadic lives, popping in and out of New York City and the country, but they touched down in Lower Manhattan and made their presence felt.

The original Beat circle was still cooking, still publishing books, still giving readings, gathering in lofts filled with jazz and reefer smoke. The Poetry Project readings hosted by Saint Mark's Church often had star-studded line-ups. Everyone was in town and in their bones. The subway trains were splashed with multi-color graffiti. The emphasis on art, music, and culture was coming to a head.

SEPTEMBER 25TH, 1979

I've been writing about experiences scoring street dope on the Lower East Side. Haven't shown these cleaned-up pages to Bill yet. Gave Howard Brookner a ten-page scene. Will see how he responds. Meanwhile, I will scrutinize what I have because I do want Bill to see it soon.

TUESDAY OCTOBER 2ND, 1979

Just learned Manor Books is dropping its paperback book line and will be publishing only magazines so no more of those formulaic erotic novels, but it's gonna hurt our production. I was group captain over two monthly paperback lines and they both just cut. Got to scramble to find new accounts and with the tech so different it will be hard.

I saw Kenneth Anger's Magical Lantern Series in a movie house in the West Village and reported to William that Anger himself was in the theater. He had given a little talk after the films. I expressed admiration for a few of the flicks, notably

Fireworks, *Kustom Kar Kommandos*, and *Lucifer Rising*.

"*Lucifer Rising* was to be the story of Aleister Crowley," William said. "It never quite worked out, or at least remains unfinished, but that was the idea. Even unfinished, it's a powerful work. Isis standing at the mouth of a cave overlooking a steep cliff. Blood on the Moon. Osiris cracks his staff and lightning splits the sky. A few more cracks and the moon breaks through the clouds. Anger assumes you know the story and offers no plot, but there's a unified vision running through all his films. Anger said demons were fucking him over on *Lucifer*. Demons, maybe, but he wasn't doing himself a whole lot of good either. He picked up an inept cameraman, his demon lover, and began with enough funding to just get rolling. A recipe for disaster."

"*Scorpio Rising* is the one everybody talks about, but they're all very good. Not the usual approach."

"Indeed, Anger's films are magical spells, designed to work into your subconscious."

"Too bad the subconscious mind can't be triggered like the conscious mind."

"Of course it can."

"How?"

"Do nothing. Only secret to tapping the subconscious mind is Do Nothing. This corresponds to the Buddhist thing somewhat. I don't know if 'trigger' is the right word."

"Sometimes your writing shoots straight

through to the subconscious. Is there a precise way you are doing it?"

"If there was, I'd do it all day long." He looked thoughtful for a moment. "A matter of technique, which might be very simple for one usage, and layered with complexity for another. Random elements can be tuned to a precise impact. The receiver doesn't have to take in everything at once. An accumulation of repetitive fragments leads to a whole picture. That's why you've got advertising jingles floating around in your head. You've heard a bit here and there. Your head pieces it together. Anything that goes in on a subliminal level gets processed. If you're not paying attention, in it goes. No conscious monitoring or filtering... no static. Man, you don't even know that you know it."

"Not an easy thing to bring to the page."

"An aspiration perhaps." Bill looked thoughtful. "I can see where *Lucifer Rising* would present a challenge. Who would play the Great Beast?"

"Take some stature... Orson Wells," I guessed.

"Mohammad Ali."

"Or maybe go the other way. Some wimpy little fuck with a whining voice."

"A wimpy fuck in Bermuda shorts with a booming boardroom voice."

"Bermuda shorts, earflaps. Nose always red and runny. Do you need the conscious mind later, to deal with what's emerging from the subconscious?"

"I think the conscious mind will eventually be phased out as a failed experiment. Think of it, no conscious ego. Just tear all that negativity out of human interaction."

THURSDAY OCTOBER 5TH, 1979

John cooked a great dinner: pasta, artichokes, chops. Bill ate the center out of two chops, pushed the plate away, and attacked the jellybeans. He had a habit of wolfing down the center of the chops, then pushing his plate away and reaching for the sweets. He washed it all down with a fresh vodka and Coke and John smiled. He'd learned to roll with this.

William looked oddly pleased with me. "Howard says I should see what you've been writing lately. You have it with you?"

"Oh no, I'm still cleaning up the 30 pages I have and expanding it a bit. Howard only has the first 10."

MONDAY, NOVEMBER 5TH, 1979

William was fresh from the set of the movie *Heartbeat* when my partner Al, Victor, and I picked him up at Kennedy Airport in Al's big Caprice. I gave him a loaded weeper and he booted a good strong fix in the car. We hit the road Bunker-bound with a Billie Holiday cassette on, plenty of good smoke, and a relaxed mood in the big Yankee wheel.

Victor provided pre-mixed cocktails as he prompted William to talk about his adventure. We knew *Heartbeat* was to be the story of Jack Kerouac and Neal Cassady. We were hungry for details.

Bill wasn't sure how he felt about the in-progress film. "Nick Nolte was most impressive as Neal. Twitchy, jumpy. Had him down. Problem with this sort of treatment is it can alter things in the marketplace. If it goes over, interest heats up. If it doesn't make it, industry people will avoid any related material for a long time."

"What was Hollywood like?"

"The people making *Heartbeat* put James and I up in a nice pad. Nice car, all the reefer we wanted. One cat took me aside and laid a piece of Mexican mud on me. An ill-processed black goo. Hit just fine. Problem with an unrefined product is the alkaloids are in crude form. Heroin of course, but also morphine, opium. Best results come from a refined material. Oh well, did the job."

"Was the story pretty accurate?" Victor asked.

William shrugged. "I wasn't in the States for much of that period. For all I know... I got a chuckle out of a scene in a Chinese restaurant when the Ginsberg character stands up and announces, 'Waiter, there's a turd in my soup.'"

I had some new pages to give William to read but decided the time wasn't right. He'd settle in and get back in a routine. Maybe I'd do another draft before presenting a new story. I was playing around with a collection of shorties called *Price of Function*. I had a dozen stories but only one or two were presentable. And the pages Howard saw had grown a bit beyond his reading.

A few nights later, I was invited over for dinner and packed the pages in my bag. The Bunker had an eerie quietude, and William was in a strange mood. John came down. He was cooking dinner. Chops, artichokes, greens. John and William tossed down a few cocktails while I sipped a Coke and rolled reefers. I never particularly liked alcohol and certainly had enough problems without cultivating a taste for it.

"What happened to David?" Giorno asked Bill. David Prentice, a painter friend, had been invited.

A strange atmosphere accompanied William as he touched his chin thoughtfully, as if formulating an answer to some deep mystery. We're sort of hypnotized, waiting for him to say something. Then the fridge kicks in with a loud buzzing noise. Bill moves his hand from his chin. The buzzing stops. John and I crack up laughing.

"What? Is something funny?"

John and I were still eating when William dug into the gumdrops.

"How do you feel about solitude?" I asked.

"Oh? What brings that up?"

"I just read the section of *Thus Spoke Zarathustra* where Z returns to the mountain and is confronted by Solitude, who says something like, 'So, it ain't pretty down there. To walk among men is to be betrayed. They don't want the truth. They want... consideration.'"

"Stormy little Kraut, that Nietzsche." He lit a Senior Service and exhaled, obviously thinking this over. "Solitude is great for a writer. But if you want living material you've got to get off your ass and go down the mountain to get it."

"Do you ever feel too alone?"

"Not really. Everyone I've ever known is with me... all the time."

It was a great dinner complete with those chilly silences only Bill Burroughs could muster. I was learning how to sit there and listen. It took effort not to blurt out something just to break an eyeball-bombing session. But if you braced yourself and maintained silence, those dangerous peeps would eventually move along.

After dinner we went into the archive room and fired the blowgun at a target William made from an old box.

Wzzzzzp!

Right before leaving I handed William the envelope with my pages in them. "This might be a short story. I'm hoping it's the opening of a novel but can't tell yet. Just a few more pages than Howard saw."

"Good. Give me a week."

I understood my pages had to wait while he worked on his own. It amazed me that he always found the time, eventually, to get back to me and say exactly the right thing.

It had been a week since Leslie called from Paris. She walked into the office just as the dayshift was packing to leave. It was Friday night. The building was emptying out for the weekend. I knew her primary role in life was torturing me, but she looked so bright and sexy. It was good to see her.

"So how'd it go?"

"I hate modeling," she spat.

The office was totally quiet. We were alone. She'd brought back a few grams of French smack but had none on her. It was in her safety deposit box and she couldn't get to it until Monday. I broke out some opium from my office stash. She dropped a gram. I did a mere quarter gram. Soon we were rolling doggie-riffs on the futon.

Next day I was innocently sitting in the office when James and Howard walked in. James had flown in from Lawrence to do some work with Bill. He was often a stabilizing influence but this time he was simply not up to it. In fact, he went into a long reverie about jerking off into Dynel wigs. He then grabbed a bolster pillow and began fucking it, much to the amusement of our associates and staff. In a burst of inspired madness James made it vividly clear that if not properly nourished with high-quality exotic leaf this instant, he would tear out onto Fifth Avenue and present himself to the first attractive mammal that passed by, demanding penetration! We managed to restrain him.

Howard and I were begging for mercy as laughter was entering that painful zone where you're a bit scared. Your breathing is weird, heart pounding, ribs rippling, cool sweat. Howard and

I had a problematic wrinkle in our rapport when it came to laughter. If something had been funny ten minutes ago, we just had to look at each other and we'd start crackling and cackling all over again.

That evening William gave me a copy of a limited edition of *Port of Saints*. He inscribed it: "For Stewart with all best wishes and friendship from all the Saints. William S. Burroughs." Under the words he drew a calligraphic design of simple delicate lines with a brush-effect pen. A few days earlier, he'd given me a copy of *Cities of the Red Night*.

That evening walking Bowery up to East 21st Street, I had a long and vivid daydream, personnel provided by memory chips and reconstituted pebbles:

I am back on Brooklyn's blood-red brick arteries with my first real girlfriend, Cesia. Wide avenues, narrow streets, low buildings, white sky. We turn a corner onto a snowy afternoon street a million years ago. Girl magic. Eyes sparkling. Snowflakes falling softly, glinting on her hair and cheeks. Cold pale winter skin. The air alive with frost and steam. All the intensity of a first love in those vivid pictures from the files: reconstituted but firm in time and place. You never fully leave. 1962. The rise above Sunset Park at 9th Avenue. But I know if I go back there, I will be alone...

I do go back. Sunset Park, Redhook, Flatbush, East New York, Brownsville, Ocean Hill. The ever-fading apparitions who composed my youth are forever with me. I perambulate. I see them coming on the street, until they get close enough for focus and reconfigure into strangers. I see them in my head, sharp and clear and near. On patrol through the old nabes I can feel their vapors in the timeless emanations.

Things had settled into a pattern. Howard had just returned from Europe and was again deep in his editing project. He still had shooting to do, but was determined to get on top of what he had so he could integrate new footage without going nuts.

William had decided to cool the supply pressure that junk was placing on him by purchasing some excess methadone from Herbert Huncke. Huncke was a five-star Methadonian of long standing and had accumulated take-home privileges despite endless infractions in the form of "dirty urines." Given the rules that govern Methadonia, Huncke was a one-man crime wave. Multiple threats to suspend take-home doses, verbal reprimands. Still, the industry poured the goodness down his throat. He was on a drop-dead dose. One hundred milligrams daily. The average junkie would be sucking his toes for two days. Herbert managed to siphon off a hundred plus mills weekly for Louis' daily ten and whatever else he could sell. Bill gave him one hundred bucks, causing Huncke to gladly part with a full sealed bottle every week. Huncke probably didn't feel any discomfort. On a saturation dose you can skip a day without much fuss, especially if you're on Huncke's side trip Rx of cocaine and valium. I don't know if he ever handed in clean pee. If he did, it was someone else's. At any rate this methadone stash allowed William to feel secure, and if the street was too hot for scoring or he couldn't spend the money to pick up, he had something to hold him. And Huncke was pleased to be a weekly guest at the big table, if only for commerce and a half hour of William's company.

It wasn't long before Bill's stash became a community safeguard. One morning I picked William up at Kennedy Airport. I explained that Manhattan South Tactical Police were out hard and heavy and scoring had been impossible. I had no stash to greet him with and was more than a touch junksick. As soon as we settled down in the car, he pulled out a methadone bottle and administered a few drops for my comfort.

"Alright Stew, we're approximating of course, but I'd say this is a good twenty. Let's find a place to grab a bite before aiming back to the Bunker."

"Good idea. I hate to drive when I'm sick."

I pulled into a diner and we relaxed over sandwiches and coffee.

Back at the Bunker, William was unpacking when the phone rang. I picked it up. It was James making sure Bill got in alright. William spoke to him for a while, then made a few phone calls.

"Stick around for dinner," he suggested. "Huncke's coming over. Louis Cartwright is going to show a short film he made. John and James are due any minute."

A short while later the table was full of faces and the methadone was kicking in nicely. I sat rolling a few joints.

"This film is called *Nuclear Scorpions*," Louis announced as he started the projector. The flick consisted of William, Allen Ginsberg, and Huncke sitting around the same bunker table we were sitting at, talking. It was jerky and twitchy. Their rapport was more interesting than anything said. Old friends, everyone firmly in their roles. More playful than profound. There were patterns to their interactions that had solidified over the years. Something about Allen triggered William to act as if he had two feet on the ground, which was hardly the case. Allen would bring forth a utopian ideal—maybe socialism or communism—and Bill would shoot it down. Huncke would issue his hoarse wise laughter and listen attentively, ever alert to anything that might trigger his sensitivity. He always seemed on the verge of being offended or conversely apologizing and breaking into his Humble Pie Routine. He knew Allen as an eternal patsy and William as a hard case who didn't want to hear him kvetch. There was often a discord in the air, largely due to Huncke's eternal scuffling for a buck. He saw Allen and Bill as rich guys who had employed him as underworld guide without proper compensation. Resentment bubbled just under the surface. It leaked out occasionally.

When the flick ended, I was surrounded by the same voices except Allen's was missing. Giorno and James filled in the gap. It was a strange feeling. As if the transition was partial and unreal.

Huncke told me he got on methadone in the very beginning, when the government dramatically expanded programs to treat heroin-addicted Vietnam vets returning to the States. "In those days they'd start you off at one-fifty or even two hundred milligrams." His eyes sparkled. "The purity those 'Nam guys were using was serious. The object with methadone is to establish a blockage dose, where you're blocked from feeling heroin. Two hundred milligrams man, you're not gonna feel much of anything." He let out his ancient laugh.

"So why not use heroin to block you from feeling more heroin?"

Huncke smiled. "Exactly, lad, exactly."

"So does your dose do it for you?"

"I settled in at a hundred mills. That's more than I need. Maann, runnin' a habit in New York City is a young man's game. I don't want the hassles of stealing and copping, and I don't want to go back to prison. I did almost fifteen years. Not straight. Five here, five there. Been in all the upstate prisons... except the honor farms. The methadone will have to do it. I buy some valiums occasionally. Do a little coke. No dope. Not much point to it. I'd have to do a lot to even feel it."

"You obviously like a little pot."

"When I can get it. Louis has a guy he scores from. Louis works in this deli in Brooklyn Heights and one of his customers sells him nickels. Nothing like what I see you're smoking but it's decent."

I found Huncke engaging enough to set up a lunch with him near my office. Bill had cautioned me. I was not flying blind.

THURSDAY, NOVEMBER 22ND, 1979

Thanksgiving dinner with William and Victor at One Fifth, Mickey Ruskin's. Victor was telling Bill about "The Kid," as Tom Sullivan was called. Bill looked at me and said, "I don't think a new dope contact is necessarily a good thing."

I was wondering about that. At the end of November I'd be turning 32. I knew it was time to walk away from dope, but often it seemed impossible. Business pressures, pressure to write, the crazy roller coaster of day-to-day life. It often seemed counterintuitive to stop using. My head was far from clear on the subject.

One afternoon I'd picked up a bundle of Dr. Nova on Rivington Street and made it over to the Bunker. Bill was grateful. He'd been on edge and was out of Huncke's magic juice. The Old Doc could not cop on the street. He was too white. The Puerto Ricans just waved him on. "Beat it j'bad company. Keep walkin'."

Once we were driving back from Kennedy Airport and he wanted dope, so I rolled over to Eighth Street and Avenue D, where the activity went 24/7. I spotted a scrambler I knew, Rene, and waved him over. As he got near the car he saw Bill. Three-piece suit and tie, gray chilly face.

"Sorry poppa. Take it outta here."

"So how was your lunch appointment with Huncke?" Bill asked, as we settled in at the big table.

"Well, he showed up at my office with the manuscript of *Guilty of Everything* and even did a spontaneous reading for my associates and workers. A demented little fairytale about tricking on the Deuce in the 1940s. Everyone was charmed."

"Charmed out of their pants, I'm sure. I gave him that title, *Guilty of Everything*. It began as an observation and became a title."

"As he got up to leave a strange thing happened."

"Oh?"

"Well, my partner Al and his friends were hanging out in the small private room, and everyone was smoking a lot of boo. They start playing Top Dog Potlatch. One dog pulls out a sticky sweet multi-color bud of red and gold Calif. 'Let's get toasted.' Then another dog exhibits a corked narrow test tube with a long bud of golden copper Thai leaf pressing the Pyrex. Dog Three extends a ball of 'shish from India. We were doing some serious smoking. Whew. At some point I gave Huncke an ounce of some reasonably good shit. Not exotic but smokable. You know, don't cost me much. He was very grateful. *Thank you thank you thank you don't fuckin' mention it already.* Suddenly his face crinkled with concern and he and started tapping himself all over. He said, 'Oh man, what happened to that ounce?' Me and Al start running our hands along the pillow bottoms, lifting up the sofa and futon—"

William started to laugh. "Oh, I see."

"—I figured hell, it'll turn up somewhere. I'll just lay another on him and find the one he lost later. And I was about to dig back into the stash when Al said, 'Hey Herbert, pull up your cuffs.' Herbert did and there was the missing ounce bulging out of his sock. No one looked more shocked than Herbert."

"Shocked he was!"

"So... do you think he knew it was there all along?"

"I think he almost walked out of your office with two ounces."

"You told me to be careful. Still—"

"I'd go easy on getting him too chummy with your Brooklyn friends. You don't want to be fitted for a body bag. Unless you give them the full disclaimer and make it clear they're on their own. You're not responsible for any bad magic that might result in exposure to the Huncke Corporation."

"That's a mouthful."

"Yes, yes... amen. Amen already."

"Are we talking outside of any expectation of ethics we might acknowledge as reliable?"

"Huncke? His ethics are rigid. Rigidly criminal. Once he was set up by narcs and facing time. Junksick, no money or family to fall back on. They tried to get him to entrap Allen and me. Maybe a few others too. Huncke warned us instead. He would not roll over. We left town. He went to prison."

"Still, stealing from friends lacks integrity—"

"Well, it's a different way of seeing the world. The integrity of a thief. See man, Huncke would never steal from someone who has less than him. As far as he was concerned, Allen and I and our whole circle were the rich Ivy League set. We were using him. In a sense he was liberating us. He knew his way around Times Square, knew the jazz scene from the inside, the streets, about scoring dope and scuffling. He was introducing us to people and to a way of seeing the world. He was using us in turn. Lifting a rug I had stored in Allen's closet and selling it to buy dope. Sneaking a few rare books out of Allen's apartment and offing them to a rare book dealer. Allen received the worst of it because he could not bring himself to stay mad at Huncke for these infractions. Whereas I made it clear that this kind of thing would not be tolerated."

"Your friendship has endured."

"I believe a mutual respect has evolved. Now that he's on the methadone program he's more prone to profiting than pilfering. I give him a hundred bucks a week for one bottle of meth. Still, I would not leave him alone in the archive room for five minutes. He's aware of this and always acts a bit insulted. A very sensitive guy, Mr. Huncke. A strong and highly specialized talent for locating schmeck anywhere. Man, he could score in the Gobi Desert."

"Sure, Bill. Some camel jockey racing by would smell his yen and pause to negotiate a blessing."

An old Jewish wiseguy I knew from Flatbush called the office one morning. He was working with the Litho Company I'd agreed to write or produce pulp novels for. Stosh put them onto the idea of erotic pulp which he called "fuck books" and now instead of four printer-ready packages a month they wanted eight. I groaned but agreed. I had a good pool of writers and it would cover office expenses. The next day the gent's sideman met me for lunch at Pete's Tavern on Irving Place and caked me up for the whole group. No contracts. In fact, no paperwork at all. Just the checks. On a handshake. He gave me a full month to deliver.

I put other matters on hold and went to work. Assigned writers and even broke out the Dictaphone. I could do one package every two days on tape. But after two I'd be scrambled and need rest. I took our five-star typist off another project and put her on this one.

Howard and Steven Lowe decided to write a few and managed to but it was a strain. I passed through Steven's digs on Bleecker Street just west of Bowery, right by CBGBs. I found the two of them sweating it out on two typewriters. Steven was blowing reefers. They were both bug-eyed from hooting lines of coke to keep energized while producing two titles. I watched them suffer for a while, then pointed out that they were making twelve hundred bucks on the project and probably spending that much on cocaine. It was a thought, they conceded. Nothing to worry about. Steven told me William had popped by on his way downtown the other day and hit the keyboard, filling up a few pages for them.

"Yeah, Bill wrote a sex scene for him," Howard added.

"What pages? Where are they?"

Steven pointed to a stack of manuscript pages. "In there somewhere."

Howard whipped his fingers in the air over the keyboard. "This is torture, Stew. How the hell do you pump out this bullshit?"

I performed a modest shrug. "I don't think about it much. It's a formula."

Stosh's nasty deadline took all my attention for a few weeks but a few good things happened. I managed to have dinner at the Bunker one night with William, David Prentice, Giorno, Bockris, James, and Howard. Giorno cooked a great meal. Victor gave Bill a Joseph Conrad novel. I was very blasted and much of the incident has turned into a cheerful haze.

Bill was not drinking, partially because of the other good thing that happened. A little O had come in. Just a few ounces, but cheap and strong.

James and I were talking over Bill's situation. He was using but writing, so it was hard to judge what was going on. James said, "Shouldn't be too surprised. The old junkie went home to junk." I don't think he blamed me for this. That large piece of O certainly didn't help but there was dope on the scene before the O arrived.

And after all what did I know about these things? This was my first habit. I'd played around as a kid but always had a healthy respect—or fear—when it came to junk. Too good to be true, that shit. There had to be a catch. I saw undead wafting through the old Brooklyn nabes and it wasn't pretty. I couldn't say exactly why I lost my fear at age thirty-two. Maybe the writer in me needed to summon an abomination and tapped Dark Lord Morphio for the role. I didn't have a sacrifice so it had to be me. I also lacked a spell of banishment or even containment. That would come but it would take many years. Suddenly the Sacred Substance was all around me and the people doing it were not just street sludge. The art scene, the literary scene, the music scene... it was all infected with lotus. Anyway, Bill was the master of these matters. If he got a habit he must have wanted it to happen. Dope was like a B-Complex vitamin injection straight into his writing arm. And since James was spending most of his time in Kansas, all restraints were off.

Huncke appeared at my office later that week. I got there and found Herbert and Al blowing a reefer in the private room. Al was telling him about the night before. We'd been at the Bunker and spent two hours blasting tin cans with Bill's air pistol.

Herbert dropped a valium with some Coca-Cola and got all loosie goosie. He knew I liked hearing Burroughs stories and when I asked about New Waverly, Texas, in the mid-to-late 1940s, he lit up.

"Old New Waverly or new New Waverly?"

"Start anywhere."

"Well, Bill, Joan, and the kids had to leave New York City because of Bill's legal problems. He was facing more than just a dope bust. Forging a script, I believe. It might've been over that business with Lucian Carr. I simply don't remember. Anyway, Bill's brother or maybe it was his father flew in from the Midwest and the family coughed up some cash to get him out of it. But they insisted he leave the drug scene, which meant New York City. Bill selected New Waverly, Texas, and off they went."

"Why New Waverly?"

"He had an old boyhood friend who knew the area. They were going to make a fortune crop farming. Of course, Bill thought he'd grow some pot. That's when he called Allen Ginsberg in New York and requested my presence. He wanted me to score some pot seeds and make it to Texas. I was strung-out and broke, so when Allen told me, I jumped on it."

"You must have been flattered to be invited."

"I don't think Bill invited me because he was particularly fond of me. He wanted a companion for Joan, and he wanted to grow pot. I was supposed to bring the seeds but typically fucked up and left them in New York. Bill was not very happy about it and that's how our renewed friendship began. Joan and I always got along famously. She was mannered, accommodating, brilliant, and had more imagination than anyone in that crowd, up to and including her husband. She had a very cerebral orientation and a wide variety of interests. Bill always needed people like that around him you know."

"What could be better for a writer than interesting companions?"

"I don't think he connected with her the way she did with him. He was crazy about her, but there was a lack of sympathy in some areas, which I found annoying. He rarely helped with the kids or around the house. Joan managed to ride with it. Bill could be charming."

"Was he protective of her?"

"Usually. Although she was certainly off on her own when it came to her drinking and amphetamine use." He laughed. "You've reminded me of something. One night, maybe a year before New Waverly, Bill and I were in a Times Square joint—I think it was called 'the Terminal Bar'—on the Deuce, tossing down shots. A little further down the bar this huge drunken moron was abusing his date. Barking at her, slapping her. Bill kept glaring but the guy wasn't facing us and didn't see him. At some point Bill whispered: 'This has gone far enough!' He got off the barstool. He was using dope at the time and must have weighed all of eighty pounds. He walked up behind the guy and gave him a swift karate chop to the back of the neck."

"What?"

Huncke laughed. "Yeah, with all his might."

"Did the guy go down?"

"Naw, he barely noticed. He turned around to see what happened but wasn't very concerned at all. He might've said 'Yeah? Wodda ya' want?' Then he went back to barking at his date and Bill walked off nursing a sore hand."

"At least he tried."

"Yeah, ever the gentleman."

Victor walked into the office just then to show me some pictures he'd taken at the Bunker. A few of Al's friends popped in and were elated to find Huncke on set. They got a charge out of Huncke's bent take on the world. Soon reefers were firing up in every corner. The private room was right next to production and clouds of reefer smoke were leaking into the typesetting area.

Huncke kicked into hustle mode. I saw him clocking everyone's attitude, presentation, position, figuring what kind of touch they were good for. A little pot from the Rolex, maybe ten or twenty bucks from the gold ring. He decided to honor us with another private reading, get the energy flowing his way. This time I turned on the tape recorder.

He read a section from *Guilty of Everything* with such dramatic delivery that we were tempted to applaud. Instead, I gave him ten bucks as did one of Al's associates. We also laid a half of a primo Thai stick on him. These sticks were legendary and were just breaking through from the mountains of Thailand to Brooklyn and

Manhattan. Huncke made no attempt to stuff it in his sock. After a while he split.

A few nights later Victor Bockris threw a dinner party at his Perry Street digs with William, Jeff Goldberg, Legs McNeil, some Mexican cat who was lighting man for the Ramones, and another muchacho who edited something called *Smut* magazine. No doubt reporting back to the Vatican but in such deep cover he'd grown fond of issuing *Smut*.

Victor placed a huge candied ham on the table next to a serving plate of exquisitely prepared vegetables. Jeff poured the drinks. I was the only one not drinking but I kept pace with fat reefers which after a while only Bill and I were hitting. Bill's never refused a lit reefer. Just as we were sitting down to eat James arrived.

There was a structure to the evening I found interesting. Victor, Legs, and Jeff formed a circle that had long been associated with *High Times Magazine*. There was referencing going on between them that was esoteric in nature. Victor, being the ambassador, had to tie the circle into a larger Burroughsian configuration. The situation was eased of course by a mutuality of respect for the Maestro. But hey, it takes two sides to tango, and you never know how the shit will shake.

Bottles of wine quickly emptied. Much jabber. Uncle Bill proper in suit and tie sitting disdainfully across from Legs, whose elbows were on the table, as his hairy armpits protruded from his sleeveless Punk shirt. Legs had been a founding father of *PUNK* magazine and ran with the high dogs in that kennel. *PUNK* was the first readable rag to come out of that angry artistic circle. Leg was the editor. He could read and write and had a personality that set him apart.

Jeff helped Victor with the table, clearing this, replenishing that. James was in a goofy mood and had me laughing crazily. He imitated one of my office staff and had the bozo down to the slightest gesture. Bill looked on blankly.

Suddenly I knew Victor was getting a bit nervous. This dinner was important to him and he wanted everyone to have a good time but Bill looked to be on the verge of one of his famous stony silences.

Then something triggered William and he became animated, addressing me as if we'd been in the middle of a conversation and I'd been stubborn or thick-headed.

"Man, do you realize how fucked-up the white race is? Have you any *idea*?"

"Ahm—"

"Pregnant with evil. Flushed with it, marinated in it!"

"Did you hear about the cache of weapons found at Sutton Ho?" I blurted. Bill often did this to me: bum-rushed me with an idea. I figured he was prodding me to be good on my feet, ready for a jolt, so generally I tried to respond and say something that would extend his riff.

"What?"

Jeff perked up. "Sutton Ho, England. A Viking

ship found and excavated. Lots of artifacts."

"A Viking ship armed to the teeth," I added.

"Of course, the albino mutants had weapons, man. The white race had an army way before they had any enemies. They went out on the high seas to drum up some enemies! Think of the ruin those rampaging white devils left behind. Being demonized by the Church maybe fueled their bloodlust. After all the Vikings' Gods were older. The Ancient Ones."

"The American Indians had weapons and warfare. Why weren't they ready for the Europeans?" I asked.

"They knew about war, but it didn't do them much good. War was a simpler thing to the Indians. They didn't come near understanding God-fearing smug Biblical White Evil."

A chilled quietude hovered over the room.

"That's too general, William. What about the defectors?' I ventured.

"Defectors can be largely exempt from collective insanities. True in any society. But there are precious few." Bill looked around the room with bony blue-eyed mischief. He broke into his Wasp-Preacher-From-Hell persona. "As I was sayin' to ol' Whispering Lou from down Nigger Lynch County, God wants us to kill off them contaminated races wot're pollutin' our nation." He pounded the table. "Put the fear of the Lord in 'em, yessir!"

Victor relaxed. Bill was in a glorious mood, having enjoyed the dinner and the company. He was entertaining us and feeling good.

The dinner started to wind down. James had a date and split. William was looking tired. I had my little VW around the corner on Bleecker Street and we left together so I could roll him back to the Bunker.

A few weekends later, Victor arranged dinner at the Bunker, arriving with two fat shopping bags of food and commandeering the kitchen. He set straight to work and was buzzing around in a frantic effort to prep various ingredients so everything would be ready at the same time. Jeff was the chef of the evening and was hovering behind Victor calling the shots. Victor turned into a veritable blur of motion.

Ira Jaffe and his girlfriend Patricia arrived just as the food was ready. I called John Giorno and told him to come down and complete the table. Ira worked for a methadone clinic doing community relations: a difficult gig, as no one wants snarling whining shoplifting hubcap-harvesting undead Methadonians haunting their neighborhood. Steal the copper plumbing out from under your ass. Ira had one of those voices that carried a ring of thought and credibility. He could be convincing without resorting to volume. William had grown fond of him. He also had a deep interest in medicine, reading medical journals and texts, keeping up on what was new and improved in the croaker world. He intended, even back then, to go through medical school and become a doctor, which he eventually did.

"So Bill, are you still buying methadone from Huncke every week?" Ira inquired.

"Yes, and Mr. Huncke is more than pleased to take my money."

"You know there's a very nice private program uptown. Doctor Karkus. A celebrity clientele. Patients' visits are timed so they rarely bump into each other. Privacy is the objective. It's a hundred bucks a week but you don't sit long in a waiting room. You have an appointment. Perfect for a gentleman junkie. Come and go unseen. Very dignified. Lots of patients who are big in the arts."

"Well, it's good to know such a thing exists, Ira, but I'm not sure I want to do that. We'll see."

"It would make life easier. Let you focus on your writing instead of having to keep up a stash."

The rap made perfect sense but William wasn't buying it. "I'm thinking I might just cut the junk loose."

"Well... okay. It's a live option."

It was clearly time to change the subject. Jeff Goldberg had been reading a great deal about endorphins, which at that time were a mystery to most people. He was preparing to write a book on the subject, which was later published as *Flowers in the Blood*. He went into a scientific explanation of "the body's own Chinaman," which Bill found captivating. As usual the Old Doc was somewhat familiar with the subject but he had questions. Jeff's research made him glow with answers. As I recall, the base line on endorphins is that they are the body's own pain-killing chemicals, which fit into the brain's opiod receptors perfectly.

"Your line in *Naked Lunch* about Buddha having a 'man within' was literal," I let out.

Bill smiled. "Many of the lines in *Naked Lunch* are literal."

Leslie was getting ready to split for a one-week modeling shoot on Cape Cod so she came by to say adios. Fortunately, April was away and the crib on East 21st Street was quiet. Dreamy steam in the opium black night. Next day I drove her to the airport and on my way back to Manhattan found myself zig-zagging dreamily through Brooklyn. The old nabes. Wind off the Narrows. Memory chips waft along South Brooklyn waterfront and inland climbing Sunset Park's Mexican tempos. Through a Caribbean Flatbush, alive with commerce and streetcorner activity.

LATE 1979

With complete gratitude for William's attention to my pages, I found myself taking on further duties around the Bunker. I'd bring in dinner when Giorno was out of town or not cooking. When William was touring I'd drive him to the airport and picked him up upon return, usually with a big comfy American longiron borrowed from my Brooklyn friends. During these absences I would go to his post office box at Canal Street Station and pick up the mail. If important I'd call him from the Bunker and read it to him. The perks were that I had Bunker keys and could use the space to read, write, and get high. And I had the feeling of being useful to someone who was helping me perfect my writing style.

William needed to have creative people around him. He thrived in an atmosphere of imagination, expansion, and projection. It had always been his policy to surround himself with a symbiotic support system and I felt fortunate to be incorporated into the design. We all had our places. Howard was filming his documentary, and also functioned as a blade runner, which was our term for going out in the field to score. Victor was writing his book on Burroughs and arranged dinners with interesting people. This was an important function as William was fussy about who appeared at his table. James edited Bill's pages and provided a household and a trusted aide. Giorno, a poet and great cook, was perfect companionship and often opened for him at readings. Because I owned a business and had a cash flow, I became the guy who could get hold of a big ride and drive William to a reading or the airport or give him a quick loan from the corporate account (which he always paid back without being asked).

One day William hosted Allen Ginsberg, Peter Orlovsky, and John Giorno for dinner. I hadn't been out of the safe house for weeks and looked forward to it.

I put on a fresh shirt and sports jacket, twinkled up a joint of Thai weed with a dusting of

Goodness, and walked slowly across the lawn to the car. It was a beautiful crisp early evening, and the setting had an unearthly calm to it.

I arrived at the Bunker to find Bill's guests in place. Allen Ginsberg had appeared earlier with a bag of Chinese takeout, which now formed the centerpiece on the big table. He and Bill were enjoying each other's company as Peter laid out dishes and silverware. Giorno mixed pre-dinner cocktails. William went for the usual Coca-Cola and vodka.

Professor Ginsberg was on a roll. The subject matter pulled me right in. He was suggesting that televised evangelism be criminalized on the same grounds as LSD. "These programs and the ideas they present encourage hallucinations, incite visions, illusions of grandeur and self-righteous acts of violence."

"That's a lot to put on religion," Orlovsky protested.

"Religion is the engine that drives many highly principled acts of mass carnage," Bill chimed.

"Amen!"

"It's the Devil's work they do!"

Allen chuckled. "Hey. Bill and I agree on something for a change. He's not shooting down my extravagant statements with his crotchety critiques."

"That's because you are not proselytizing socialism or its naked and no-good nephew commmmmmunism at me. I don't disagree with you merely for sport."

"I'm not so sure."

"Gee Allen, you are kind of tormentable," I injected.

"I must be. I don't hear Bill bickering with anyone else."

"Listen here. I bicker with whomever I please." He turned to Giorno. "John, don't I bicker freely?"

John waved away the question. "I'm neutral here."

"John's Switzerland. We can deposit our funny money with him and continue enumerations." William picked up a piece of chicken on a fork and smirked. He eyeballed the chicken, then Allen. "Where did you purchase this cheap swill?"

After dinner we sat around smoking and blabbing. It was always a pleasure to see Allen and Bill interact. Allen was so obviously the student. He defended himself for a while, then demurred gracefully—if not conditionally—as William tore into him.

For reasons I can't recall, William asked me the name of the girl who answers the phone at my office. I said, "Sukey Tawdry." I don't know why. Just a goof.

"Ahh," Bill let out playfully. "And ol' Lucy Brown."

I laughed. I'd mentioned the name of a character in *The Threepenny Opera* who never even appears. Sukey Tawdry is the prostitute who hides Mac when the Law is looking for him. There is just one quick reference to her. Bill not only picked up on it but slid into a very convincing invocation of Macheath, Prince of Thieves. He darted to the kitchen sink and picked up a large glinting knife. "Tools of the trade," he cooed. He stroked it lovingly as if it were about to ejaculate. "Look out! Ol' Mack is back!"

"Of course, you know that Brecht was a socialist," Allen inserted.

"Not quite yet," Bill corrected. "On his way to Marxist dogma, certainly, but he had not yet arrived. Once committed to socialism, he never wrote anything nearly as penetrating and human." Bill extended the knife like a sword. He stabbed at the air. "Yessir. Macheath was schooled in the ways of the blade. Jab, slice, dice."

"I don't see how you could call *Threepenny Opera* a socialist play," I chimed.

"Not directly. But it is a negative statement about capitalism, which amounts to the same thing," Allen informed.

"Oh?"

"Allen's correct," Bill confirmed. "Macheath's white gloves and fancy clothes. He is amoral and bourgeois to the core. He's arranged to have an orphanage burned down as a political favor. He's jacking people left and right, wiping their blood off his blade." Bill took a dishrag and wiped the long filero. "A dashing figure, capable of anything if the price is right. Who is better suited for success in a capitalist system?"

"And the play ends with Mac's arrest and

full pardon," Allen added. "He was just too well-mannered to prosecute. Lie, cheat, kill. As long as you dress right and display appropriate charm."

"To do that today you'd need a public relations man. Ol' Uncle Ivy Lee could get on the phone and tighten you up." Bill put down the blade. "Clean up your image. Have you fucking knighted."

"Macheath was a saint compared to your Uncle Ivy," Allen let out.

"Ivy Lee was merely of his time. It was the birth of the Spin."

"Spin?"

"A subtle re-writing formulated to make whatever you have done seem correct. Old man Rockefeller applied the rules of war to business. Ruthless and nasty. He'd set up blind tiger corporations to bluff the competition. They posed as independents but were under his orders. When he said he was going to 'standardize' the oil industry it was pure spin. He meant he was going to own it. And Standard Oil did just that. No anti-monopoly laws yet. A pitiless game plan. Once he was successful, his image had to be softened. Ivy Lee stepped up and turned him into a benevolent ol' grandpa giving out shiny dimes to the kiddies."

"A sweet old man," Allen added.

"With the smell of death—and not his own—hovering gently in the air."

"So much for capitalism," Allen blurted.

Bill threw out a look that ended this patter and set the stage for a long pregnant silence. It was broken only with some Burroughsian reportage concerning one Louis Cartwright. "Did you hear what happened to Louis and Herbert?"

"I can only guess," Ginsberg let out.

Bill went on with gleeful amusement. "They were in that longshoremen's bar on Atlantic Avenue in Brooklyn, down by the waterfront. Louis got into a little miff with someone. Not hard to imagine, hey Allen? Well, instead of duking it out mono-to-mono, Louis pulls out a can of mace and sprays his noble challenger."

"Of all the limp-dick pussy-faced moves!" I spit.

"Indeed. While effective, this gesture put him and Huncke on the shit-list of both patron and proprietor. Their occluded assholes are no longer welcome in this establishment."

"Well, there are other bars in Brooklyn, Bill."

"Watch Louis burn them down one at a time. I don't know how Huncke puts up with him."

"And who else would put up with Huncke?"

"Yes. That's as close to an explanation as one can hope for."

"Huncke's methadone clinic is right around the corner from my East 21st Street crib," I informed. "When I was staying there, he'd drop in on me regularly. He'd come in all bright-eyed, sit down on the sofa and give out a yarn or two. Then he'd melt as the methadone kicked in. A few times I walked down Second Avenue with him and it was an experience. Every panhandler addressed him as 'Mr. Huncke.' A ragged junkie rattling a cup full of change receives a pocket-tapping demonstration followed by a brow-wrinkling apology. 'I wish I had a quarter to lay on you, maaan. Or even a dime. Maybe I've got an extra smoke for you.' Another pocket-tapping and another apology. 'I'm sorry. I'm probably more broke than you are right now.' He'd go on and on until the poor skid got sick of it and backed off. 'Okay enough already.'"

Allen and Peter left, and things quieted down.

Leslie knew where I was and fell by. She knew William was fond of her and would be welcoming. Bill was in a grand mood. He was imagining a political movement based on the premise that "Junk Is Beautiful!"

"We junkies have been shat upon long enough! We are getting tired of this treatment. Let us gather yon junkies into a voting bloc, a 'bund' if you will. Let's accumulate fearless operatives ready to sacrifice life and limb for the cause. Then we go out lookin' for converts. 'Have a sniff. Isn't it yummy?' We will rapidly swell into a national or even international power making big demands on the status quo. Give us our medicine! We want it cheap! Strong! Ready for the cooker!"

He was all lit up like a TV preacher. I mean, it was hard to doubt the sincerity fueling his tongue and those big white-devil blue eyes earnest with the fever.

After we got high, he told us about his recent decision to go on the methadone program. "Ira Jaffe has arranged for me to meet with Doc Karkus uptown and see about enrolling in his high-toned celebrity clinic. A discrete arrangement. Karkus plans carefully timed appointments, so you don't bump into your fellow lepers. No one sees you doing the walk of shame in and out of his office."

"Sounds reasonable," I said. I knew Ira had been pushing for William to go on the program as a means of dealing with his re-addiction. I also knew Bill was not going to stop opiates. At his age it would have been no easy trick. Besides, he was writing. He was happy. And Ira had found a way for Bill to do it without being too public about the matter.

"Scoring dope all the time is just too expensive and disruptive. I'm buying methadone from Huncke every week, Stew. Might as well do it right. Ira is making it easy. Get on a gentleman's dose and go back to my pages."

"But wouldn't you prefer dope to methadone?" Leslie asked.

"Prefer the white Goodness to that petroleum-based tribute to the Third Reich? Of course. It's just not practical. "

"'There is no enemy as harsh as Reason,'" I injected. "That's from *Don Quixote*. A paraphrase. Always liked that scene, where the Black Knight of Reason confronts Quixote and the friendly prince warns the Don not to joust with such a potent foe."

"That is a great book. He does joust with Reason, right?"

"Oh yes he does. Not one to back away from a fight, the Don. He stands tall. Reason drops him on his ass."

"The Quixote goes beyond greatness," William added. "We are talking about a quest. Nothing as contrived as a plot. Motion provides circumstance. The individual goes out there, actively seeking his own unique vision. In effect, bending the world to his vision. Does he land on his ass? Of course. So what?"

"Was it considered a novel?" Leslie wondered.

"There was not yet such a thing as 'The Novel,' and certainly not an 'Epic Novel.' These things evolved later. *Don Quixote* had a large impact on world literature. It's two books written about ten years apart and eventually published as one. The printing press was a recent invention."

At that moment the Bunker phone rang. Bill nodded for me to pick it up and I did. It was from the safe house. All that was said was, "Okay Specs, you'd better be on point."

"Was that Jacques Stern?" William asked

"Now it was for me. I have to get back to work."

Dinner at the Bunker a few nights later. Jeff Goldberg and James were in attendance. David Budd, Bill's painter friend, had been there but left. I was sorry I missed him. Budd had spent time on the road and had a splendid carny vocabulary, which he would break out for special occasions. He'd say shit like, "Weeeezut's heezapnin?" He knew every bunko game ever played.

Bill gleefully filled us in on the methadone

clinic run by Doc Karkus for gentlemen junkies. "Comfortable waiting area, and you sit there all alone, usually for not more than a minute. Nurse and staff are friendly. You don't see much of the Doc or anyone else. Clients are shy about bumping into each other and appointments are scheduled to protect your anonymity. They keep springing these piss tests on me, man. The nurse puts on her apologetic face and hands me the little plastic bottle. Who the hell can pee on demand? What I do is, I have an extra cup of tea in the morning, then ride uptown on the train with a bladder full. All that tea sloshing around in your gut. It's not the most comfortable thing in the world. Still an easy score. See, they won't medicate you until you give urine. If you absolutely refuse to give pee, they will medicate you, but it counts as a dirty. You might get called in to see Karkus for a verbal reprimand. Too many dirties and they limit your take-home bottles."

"I thought the Karkus op was less uptight."

"Well, I'm still new. They must watch me carefully and get to know me a little before they start increasing my take-home privileges. What do you think they are, dope pushers? Maybe I have been a naughty boy." Bill made his naughty boy face: a pouty chin-down eyes-up plea for sympathy with a touch of sarcasm leaking out.

"So they'll ease-off on the piss tests eventually, hey?"

"Well, provided I consistently produce clean urines."

It was a pleasure to be at the Bunker for the first time in weeks. As 1979 drew near the end, William was spending more time in Lawrence, and it became apparent he would move there. The tight circle around William knew changes were in the air. When William spent more than a week in New York he complained about missing his cats and the quiet of the Midwest. I walked in on Bill and Victor having dinner. Bockris promptly filled an extra plate.

They were doing some editing work on Victor's *A Report from the Bunker*. This promised to be an important work, reaching beyond the image of Doc Benway and presenting Bill Burroughs as himself. The book consisted mainly of taped and transcribed conversations, fitted into dinner parties. Sometimes the playback was inaudible, leading to mistakes which required correcting. I enjoyed watching their collaboration as they pored over a stack of pages. I sat silently as they notated.

After an hour or so they took a break. Bill performed a great routine, entertaining Victor and I with his friendly methadone counselor persona. "Now I been at it a long time, seeeee? A long time. So let's get a few things straight," he rasped. "Nobody walks away. Nobody. Twenty years I never saw one fuckin' body march out of here didn't come back begging for God's Mercy, which only my signature on a medication slip can provide." Benway's nose wrinkles in distaste as the lips form a sneer. But the voice is sweet, almost like the opening of a song. "Of course you might be the first, kid. Sure, sure, you will be the very first."

Later that night I considered sleeping in the archive room. I was tired and didn't feel like driving back to Staten Island but I did.

A few days later Bill called and invited me to dinner. I got there an hour early to have some time alone with William before Huncke and Louis Cartwright were due.

"Any pages to show me, Stew?"

"Too much trauma lately. I got married when I was twenty and now it's officially over. We're separated and will be divorced within a few weeks. Moving out of East 21st Street was unsettling and where I am now is just crazy."

"What are your days like in the safe house?"

"Well, it's a wealthy quiet suburb. Narrow streets lined with landscaped estates. No neighbor interaction at all. Haven't seen a single soul walking or standing on a lawn. They're working three identical Caprice Classics so it looks like the same car in and out. The house is a comfy old Victorian. Kiggy, who's captain of the trip we're working, collects Tiffany lamps and there's one in the living room. Nice colors reflecting from a dripping design. I grew up in tenements, Bill. Never lived in a house before. It's airy and pleasant. Doing a little too much dope, but that's not something I want to confront right now. This is temporary. It'll be over soon."

"You shouldn't get too comfortable with it. I

know how it is."

Huncke and Louis arrived. Bill made cocktails and I carved the chicken and set out plates. Huncke sat smoking a reefer as William told him about Doc Karkus' methadone clinic.

"You arrive at the appointed time and get medicated instantly. Usually I'm in and out of there with my take-out bottles in ten minutes."

"Maan, that's nothing like what I endure three times a week," Huncke whined. "There's always a crowd in the waiting room and a line for the bathroom to give pee. By the time you hit the medication windows you feel like you won the lottery. Everyone getting impatient, blabbing away at high volume. While you wait the staff is giving you the eye. They nix me on extended take-homes every time I ask, pulling out my jacket and reading off a list of infractions. Not a single dirty urine goes unmentioned."

"Every pee he gives reads dirty for valium and cocaine," Louis added. He let out a short sharp laugh that sounded like an agitated seagull. "I wonder why."

Huncke glared at him for a second and Louis shrugged and smiled brightly.

Bill and Huncke started talking about Times Square in the 1940s. *Remember old so-and-so.* I watched gleefully as all the tensions that had accumulated between them over the years seemed to melt and they were back in the day.

"You were quite the tour guide, Huncke."

Huncke smiled and folded his fingers

together. "Yes well, what students you all were. I had to take you and Allen by the hand."

"Indeed. Into a brave new world."

Huncke laughed. "I don't know how brave it was." He emitted a phlegmatic laugh.

"Took the lads off-campus, did you?" I inserted.

Huncke's eyes widened gleefully. "Oh, way off-campus we went. And some of us never returned to the cozy restraints of polite behavior."

"We weren't exactly innocent before you came along, Herbert." Bill's lips puckered with a playful petulance.

"Oh I know I can't take *all* the credit."

One morning I was sitting by the bedroom window reading *Thus Spoke Zarathustra* and saw Kiggy leaving the house carrying a backpack. I knew he had an appointment with Florida Dave, who had transported the cargo and was attached to the owners, to bank him up. I watched him walk to his car. The birdies were chirping. The sun was shining. Kiggy—boss of the trip we were working—was walking across the lawn with at least a million in cash. I'd never met Kiggy before being recruited into this tightly run scenario. None of the players knew each other and when the work was over it was understood everyone would go back to their lives and not contact their fellow workers again. How strange life is, I reflected. My teacher, Mr. Burroughs, could barely pay his rent and credit card bills. A world-famous author, published in a dozen languages and known as a master American novelist, was barely getting by. It was an example of how our society punished artists or anyone who went beyond the mundane. It was not exactly bitterness I felt at that moment. Just an irony with teeth.

At any rate, I'd turned thirty-three during the past four weeks. If all went well, I could return to Manhattan soon with enough cash to settle old debts and set up a living situation. The office rent was paid for a few months, staff covered. My partners and I would have to hustle up some typesetting work in an arena that was changing. Maybe add a little publishing to our game. We knew all about cheap magazine pre-press and had some experience with printers and distributors.

1980

SUNDAY, JANUARY 13ᵀᴴ, 1980

I fell by the Bunker to find William in a good mood. He had been awarded a three-day pickup schedule from the Karkus operation, which meant he could engage in a little foolery occasionally and still issue clean urine. "It will take a bit of timing," Bill speculated. "But an occasional bang of shmoo has become an empirical prospect."

"I don't know. I hear the cut sometimes stays with you longer than three days," I warned.

"Who tests for cut? Listen man, the medical profession is not that imaginative. They are shooting for morphine, cocaine, valium, all the clichés. I've been guest medicating in Kansas occasionally and they don't bother me with urine tests as I'm not formally their patient."

"Are you sure morphine doesn't show in urine three days later?"

"Look man, what's the worst that could happen? The Doc will sit me down and say, 'Now

Mister Burroughs, you have been a naughty boy.' I'm too old for an extended verbal reprimand."

"They can make you come in more often."

"True, true. Always fuckin' with us. About time somebody stood up for us lepers. I do want things smooth at the clinic. I'm preparing to make a permanent change to the methadone clinic in Kansas City."

There was an early copy of *Cities of the Red Night* on the big table and I looked it over carefully. "Very nice," I said.

"Dick Seaver and Holt put together a fine package. I'm pleased with it," Bill said.

"So how was working with Victor yesterday, Bill?"

"We put in some long hours and there are still corrections. But *Report from the Bunker* has promise. I'm sure it will come together nicely."

"Victor works hard. He's focused."

"Yes indeed. Maurice Girodias will be by tomorrow night. You should meet him."

"Meeting with the accountant tomorrow night. Shit, running a business is a pain in the ass."

"Ah well, the price of function."

John Giorno came down from upstairs and started prepping dinner. Bill put on Brian Jones' *The Pipes of Pan at Joujouka*. Loud.

"Man, you have to blast something like this!"

We were swaying hypnotized and inebriated as William uttered: "Jacky Blue Note plays *Pipes of Pan* as the whole structure of reality goes up in silent explosions."

As we ate Bill told us about the pipers. "See man, they sit up on this high ground over the valley. They alternate between the Pan pipes and the opium pipes. When the O pipes get clogged—and it can take a while—they go down in the valley. Their counterparts below see the exodus and respond by climbing the rise and picking up the abandoned Pan pipes. See, the Pan pipes are continuous. They go and go. Meanwhile, down in the valley with those clogged up opium pipes, the mood is just fine. They can scrape out the goodness and dream off into the music. After their pipes are dry, it's back up to the high ground."

"What a life."

"Indeed..."

I sat eating and reflecting on William's statement, which I recognized from *Naked Lunch* or maybe *Nova Express*. A blue note is a bent note, common in blues: you don't hit the note directly but slide into it. Pan is the God of Panic. If the whole structure of reality goes up in silent exposures it must mean the lid already blew and no one heard or noticed it.

John had laid out a great table. Pasta, chops, artichokes. Bill ate quickly, chomping the center out of three lamb chops and pushing his plate away. Then he reached over and gobbled a handful of chocolate.

"That's all?"

"Yeah, got the chocolate chucks." Bill picked up a newspaper. He invited us to admire the striking face of a young punk who'd "executed" a police officer. "Such a handsome killer." Bill eyed the picture hungrily. "There's no such thing as a *bad* boy!"

"That guy's gonna walk tall in prison," I speculated.

"He will have many years to practice his strut," Bill added. "Probably earned himself a life sentence."

"Or two. That means you go to the grave owing one."

"They accumulate sentences to make sure you never get out. You get ten for this crime, fifty for that. Maybe a seventy thrown on top. Your ass is deep inside. Deep deep. If you have any life at all it is in your head."

"You're kicking it with your imaginary friends and ticking off the years. First you do the two life bits, then the seventy—"

"Ticking off the days is more like it. Maybe the minutes." Bill looked thoughtful. "Reminds me of a joke Huncke told me. Judge looks at the skel and says, 'Twenty years.' Guy says, 'I can't do twenty years!' Judge gives him an understanding look and say, 'That's ok, just do what you can.'"

Then he knocked me off my balance a bit and asked, "Stew, did you have imaginary friends when you were a lad?"

"Hmm, yeah, guess I did."

"Not uncommon for writers. Were you hero-prone?"

"Not really, I hope..."

He laughed. "Surely you looked up to some of the older boys."

"There were a few guys I learned many moves from. A few I looked up to. One guy, Bob Spallina, sort of taught me how to walk around. Basic shit, like if there's blood in the air don't make eye-contact with anyone until things calm down. And there was this cat, Gillespie, who was just impenetrable. I mean, no one ever got near him enough to throw a punch. They'd face off with him. Next thing they'd remember they're in the fucking ambulance."

"What?"

I laughed. "No, that's not why I looked up to him. He was tough but he wasn't a bully. He'd try to cool shit off before it came to blood on the sidewalk. Word was, if you're gonna hit Gillespie hit'm with a train or at least a truck. After a while the challengers dwindled and you got this calm that was astonishing. No one would pull beef on anyone for any reason with Gillespie around. Especially a big guy picking on a shortie. That shit did not bounce. He was a relaxing presence—"

"In a menacing way."

"Well, yeah."

"Like a trained guard dog sniffing everyone out to see who might explode. Caution is in order when it comes to heroes, Stew. Particularly when the hero incorporates strong leadership qualities. The leader often encourages us to be reactive, secondary."

"A good leader locates what you're good at

and exploits your talents for everyone's good, including your own."

"Yes, that's an ideal. But there are flaws in the final application. Leadership is strengthened by conflict and weakened by stability. The ideal climate for leadership is one of fear. A leader might stir the shit or depend on someone else to do it. An enemy is essential to the leader's status. Also to the hero's."

TUESDAY, JANUARY 20ᵀᴴ, 1980

My business partner Alan Hirsch had noticed the heavy weight of worry William carried recently, as news of Billy's health filtered in from Colorado. Al sought to lift his spirits with a special dinner. We arrived at the Bunker with a formidable arsenal of goodies. Al had three thickly cut porterhouse steaks marinating in big plastic bags and assorted ingredients for side dishes and sauces, which he went right to work on. He gave William a fat bud of stickless Thai and placed a pan of very potent sinsemilla carrot cake on the table for dessert. "But ya have to eat the steak first, Bill," he warned.

"I'll be a good boy." Bill flashed the innocent face he'd invented for his methadone counselor. When we cracked up laughing he looked surprised.

William broke up the Thai weed slowly, enjoying the tactile treat of pulling apart a fat gorgeous bud. "This smells like Heaven," he uttered, sniffing the resin on his fingers. He observed Al unpacking his knives to perform a final trimming on the steaks. "It's always a pleasure to see a professional work."

Alan was a gifted chef, even then. Later, when our typesetting business was knocked out of the box by new technology, he went to culinary school, then studied with a famous and fabulous French chef. Eventually Al became the executive chef at the Plaza Hotel's Oak Café but at this time he was just a cat who loved to cook. He must have read a lot of cookbooks and watched those cooking shows on television because everything—every ingredient, every preparation—resulted in a superb plate. He also had a thing for wine and went to auctions and specialty shops to hunt for specific vintages. I never drank wine and paid little attention but Bill's eyes lit up when he saw the bottle Al put on the table.

"Well!"

"Yeah. I was waiting for the occasion to open that one."

"Yo, is that shit fo'tified?" I goofed. "Where are the paper bags? You can't drink wine without paper bags."

"That isn't Night Train, Stew. That kind of wine you drink out of a stemmed glass," William corrected.

Because sens-cake takes a while to hit, we chipped on a small piece while Al's preparatory elaborations continued. I was afraid Bill wouldn't be hungry but the smell of cooking meat and roasting veggies did the trick.

When the steaks were on the table being carved and placed on plates, we went to work. Al took the jellybeans off the table but he really didn't have to. Bill knew what a well-prepared steak tasted like and he was down with it. It was so good he ignored his vodka and Coke for a full fifteen minutes.

I was a bit shocked to notice Bill had eaten some of the veggies as it was his habit to treat them as decoration.

Maybe an hour passed before when we stood up to stretch, bellies bulging. I began to wonder if that carrot cake wasn't a bit too strong. "Uh, I feel a bit like I'm tripping."

"Oh, it creeps up," Al assured. "This is just the beginning."

William laughed and pulled on a reefer. "Should we meet up with any pestilence we must be prepared. To the archive room, gentlemen. I will demonstrate my latest weapons acquisition: the dreaded Spitting Cobra."

We followed William into the other room, where we were cautioned to stand back as he set a box on a chair, whipped out what looked like a footlong black flat sap, and whipped it through the air. The motion caused the sap to spring open another two or three feet with a weighted tip, which smashed into the box and sent it flying.

Bill smiled. "See that? They don't even know it's coming. This little baby packs a surprise thrust, almost like a spring sword."

We moved on to a little target shooting with

an air pistol and finally to the blowgun, which spat little beaded steel darts.

"See how far the darts penetrate! A lethal weapon derived from the most basic of technologies. You are crouched in the bush and completely invisible. No glinting metal to give away your position. No explosion. No noise or smoke. And with a little poison on the tip of the dart you have a serious capacity to damage your enemy from a distance."

Bill was into it now, showing off his toys. He hefted what looked like a slim gentleman's cane and pulled it apart to reveal a long sharp blade. "Sword canes are essential to safe passage in the colonies," he assured us.

After a while I saw Bill was losing energy. He wanted to get some sleep because James was in town, and they had some editorial matters that required discussion in the morning.

Al packed up his cooking gear. He left Bill enough sens-cake and bud to inebriate a legion as well as a steak for James. We walked out onto the Bowery.

FEBRUARY 1980

It was a few days until William's birthday, but he would not be in town. He and James had gone on a reading tour. I was staying in the Bunker, my solitude broken only by Allen and Peter, who would appear suddenly to visit the archive room where Allen was working on some of Bill's papers.

Leslie was coming over in a while and the thought of banging her cheered me considerably although there would be an emotional price. Why was beauty such a torment?

One of our typesetters used to put out a little cheap rag on newsprint called *New Wave*. The next issue would be devoted entirely to Herbert Huncke and he wondered, since Huncke often fell by to see me and we appeared tight as ticks, if I could persuade him to submit some writing and allow an interview. I told him to consider paying Huncke so I wouldn't have to convince him but there was no budget for editorial. *New Wave* was a one-man op and only the printer and paper supplier got paid. But I liked the idea and brought it up to Huncke, pointing out that the publicity could do him some good.

I was sitting in the office reading Ezra Pound and blasting Muddy Waters through earphones when Huncke appeared for an interview. He acted a little apprehensive until we broke out a black tray with snowy pink Peruvian lines on it. He gunned his nostrils and prepared for some serious business. One mighty hoof and Mr. Huncke elevated into charm mode. Repeated visits to the tray periodically restored his good humor. Our questions were very broad. We said things like, "Tell us about yourself," and asked, "What was Times Square like during the 1940s?"

With warmth and only the faintest hint of suspicion in his eyes he treated us to a full-blast invocation of his soul and spirit. He never flinched even if he turned out to be the villain in his own tale. Through Huncke's jail and skid bits, his unrelenting heroin habit and eternal desperation, his victories and failures as a thief and male prostitute, he had achieved an aesthetic that provided irony and distance. He was beyond shame. Perhaps he was, as William had suggested, "Guilty of Everything." He was one of those few souls able to let it all out.

As Herbert prepared to split, I asked him to bring some photos to the next interview. He'd mentioned he had a few photos of himself by Louis Cartwright which would fit the tone perfectly. If there had been a budget and I'd had the time, I would have interviewed people who knew him in the old days to broaden the depth of the character. But we had decided on a minimalist approach. Besides, Huncke did not like the idea of me digging up dirt. If I wanted the dirt I could get it from the man himself. I put the recording in a Dictaphone and gave it to one of the typists.

The next day at the Bunker Bill was in a good mood. He was working steadily on a few projects, testing new material to be read aloud, riding a wave of positive feedback from recent audiences. *The Place of Dead Roads* was beginning to shape up.

After years of defending his work, of seeing it degraded in the press, the snide remarks, the personal insults, refusal by the Establishment to take him seriously, Bill Burroughs was finally emerging as a great American author. It was too late for him to jump and jubilate over this but there was a sense of gratification in it. A layer of respectability had been added to El Hombre Invisible.

I told him about interviewing Huncke. "Material for the *New Wave* issue on Huncke is shaping up nicely. Soon it'll go to layout. Herbert was very gracious. Such a tentative charm."

"Oh, he can be less than tentative. Especially when he needs something." Bill smiled. "Herbert likes to 'fess up... eventually. Immediately after one of his dark acts, he will deny it to your face. A few years later it's a joke. Just remember: not only will he steal your dope; he will help you look for it."

Odd how memory chips can waft in so many contradictory breezes. Huncke recollecting summer on Bill's farm in New Waverly, Texas: "It was as if we were cut off in our own fresh fragrant paradise."

And Bill's take on Huncke. "He did nothing but complain."

Recalling early February of 1980 was an endurance test. Things at the Bunker were no less stressful as word of Billy came in daily. William's son was taking turns for the worse with a consistency that was alarming and saddening. William flew out to Colorado for a brief visit. Billy had endured a liver transplant operation with tainted success. Now he was testing out his new liver by pouring booze into it. He was on a generous morphine Rx from the doctor who had performed the transplant, so drinking struck William as unnecessary, self-defeating.

FEBRUARY 8TH, 1980

Huncke likes to drop by the office, smoke a joint, and shoot the shit. Since Bill assured him I can be trusted he has been very friendly. Always leaves with five bucks and some pot. Ever gracious, humble, and entertaining. Even Al finds him hard to resist. He is also a bit more relaxed when he realizes not all my action involves typesetting. The lad is one of our own. However, he does have a way of addressing me that makes me think I'm a potential mark in his eyes, just as Bill and Allen and that whole crew had been. I see him size me up. Guy owns a business, has people working for him, writes checks, keeps Uncle Bill in boo. There's some potential going on. Well, I'm not an Ivy League college kid with a trust fund which he will find out fast if he pulls the shit he's famous for. But I should not anticipate getting stung as it will trigger it. Just keep an ear up for bullshit. I've got a skilled photographer taking shots to augment the package. A good cover is important.

FEBRUARY 12TH 1980

On the phone William tells me he's starting to check out the pages I gave him. I ask him how they're reading...

William: "The question is not 'how does it read?' but 'how will it read in fifty years?'"

Word from William: Draft of *Dead Roads* almost ready for an early assembly. March and April will be crammed with readings. He will be trying out new material from that novel. A tour has been arranged by James Grauerholz.

I'll be taking over Leslie's crib on East 22nd Street for $400 monthly but to secure that price I must pay three months in advance: quarterly payments of $1,200.

    Leslie's been flying back and forth in a frantic effort to make modeling shoots in Paris and New York, and to continue seeing friends in New York and family in Massachusetts. Since she's loving Paris and making money there I imagine she'll limit her New York time to film shoots and brief family visits. If I'm in her old apartment she can stay with me for an overnighter, freeing up money to embellish her Paris scene. This is speculation on my part. Her life is in the fast lane now. I wonder if she knows what's coming next.

Just back from the office. I've got some opium which I'd stashed in a safety deposit box and am considering a slow reduction. O makes measured dosing possible. About to move on to a new daybook purchased at Lee Shop on Greenwich Avenue today. But first dinner. Gonna walk up Second Avenue and pick up something to cook...

    On my way up Second Avenue to the butcher, I peeked into a coffee house and saw a girl I knew sitting with another girl. On impulse I went in and said hello to Michelle, who was an art student. I'd seen her up at Manor Books doing a magazine layout. The other girl was Jenny. They both lived across the street on 21st and had graduated from the School of Visual Arts, which was also on that block. I'd seen Jenny around the neighborhood and knew her vaguely as the roommate of a girl I'd been banging occasionally. But I'd never really looked at her before and this time I did. Sparkly black eyes. I knew she was an art student like Michelle and could do magazine layout. I was struck by her quietly amused presence and calm confident manner and asked if she would care to do a layout for *New Wave*. Michelle encouraged her to show me what she could do. I made it clear that pay would be minimal. *New Wave* was merely a cultural exercise. But she would be credited as art director. She wasn't quite sure she wanted to commit herself but gave me her phone number and took mine. I excused myself and went about my business.

That night in my crib I did inventory. I had a place to live, a little cash left after paying a deposit, three months up front, and taking care of loose ends on the divorce. I had a business that employed six people. It was not making a smashing profit but I drew a salary. Attempts to get clean had been punctured but not demolished. At least I wasn't using daily. I was fixing sporadically instead of constantly. Given the turmoil of my life at this point, even that was an accomplishment. I drifted off to sleep thinking about Jenny, hoping she would call me.

Jenny called the office a few days later, just in time to do the layout for *New Wave*. She arrived at the office in the early evening and put in a few hours.

I was working on a package for Playboy Press. Not the magazine, but the paperback line. We took a break together and talked. I found out she was doing a lot of freelance design since graduating from Visual Arts. I was tempted to show my interest and maybe I did, but I kept it subtle.

The next night we did a marathon session and finished *New Wave*. "The Herbert Huncke Issue." It took some long hours but the sucker was ready for the printer. During that night I learned that Jenny had been born in Tehran. Her father was a Persian Jew and her mother was Scots-Irish from Virginia. Her mom had come to New York City on an art scholarship and had been swept off her feet by this dapper international charmer who was attending NYU and trafficking in antiquities to keep his face fed. She also told me she had a boyfriend. When it hit me how disappointed I was to hear that it dawned on me that I really liked her. Disappointment must have been written across my face, but I said nothing.

EARLY MARCH 1980

Bill opened the door and ushered me to the table with childish glee. He knew I was bringing him something special.

"Stash-house duties have allowed this little indulgence," I said as I placed four glistening ounces of shiny black opium perched in white cheesecloth down on the table.

I saw Bill's eyes dancing over the opium.

"This is the beginning and end of the O," I said. "I have no way to contact the source who laid this on Kiggy for considerations given while they worked together. Kiggy laid it on me because when the trip was over every bale in that house was accounted and paid for. Very often there are a few mysteries at final count. Kiggy's about to leave the city with no forwarding info so let's not burn through it too fast."

"Hmm, well, let's put the kettle on." As he made tea he said, "I know you had to work that load to keep your office afloat. Maybe consider not doing it again. You may come to remember it as an easy buck. It was not. You were stressed out, carrying a lot of responsibility and risk. Your very freedom was on the line."

"You're right of course. Anything could have happened. I didn't allow myself to think about it."

Allen emerged from the archive room where he'd been napping. He was a bit groggy. I passed him a lit reefer and he waved it away as if it were poison. "Oh no, you are not going to do that to me again."

I laughed.

"It's just marijuana, Allen," Bill quipped.

"I'm not used to that kind of pot. How do you get any work done?"

I shrugged. It was a valid question. "The way to function on very strong bush is to smoke it constantly. If you do it occasionally it's overwhelming."

"Allen has written some of his best poems

while inebriated," Bill stated. "Isn't that true, Allen?"

"I guess you could say—"

"Certainly, your first drafts, Allen."

"Well yes, but when I'm crafting, I couldn't possibly be stoned on that strong pot."

"You must use pot correctly, that's all. You don't smoke with the idea that you will start working after you get high. You might never start. Get yourself in motion and maybe an hour into it take a few hits on a joint. It's like anything else. A little planning goes a long way."

"Any news on Mister Corso?"

"Just what you heard already. You can spend a lot of energy worrying about Gregory. He seems to land on his feet, no matter how unlikely it appears. He will push matters until they explode. The blast propels Gregory on. Then he sets up another cozy scene and once again initiates the process of demolition."

"Doesn't he get tired?"

"Endurance is his stock and trade."

"I've heard some incredible Corso stories from Huncke. Not the most complimentary."

"Yes, I can imagine."

"Corso writes some incredible poetry. He's got a self-taught idiosyncratic style that drives images right into your head."

"Gregory can be superb, Stew. At his best he is coming directly from the heart. The poet is a paradox. I suppose we shouldn't be too astonished."

*

A week later I was back at the Bunker for dinner with Giorno, Victor, Ira, Bill, and Jeff Goldberg. Jeff's an old friend of Victor's from Philly. They ran a small press together called Telegraph Books and published a series of poetry volumes, among them a Patti Smith book and an Andrew Wylie book.

Jeff filled me in on the book he was working on. "It's about man's relationship with opium and how the brain reacts to the drug."

I cut a small piece off a chunk of black goodness and handed it to him. I'd just dropped a half gram and it was coming on.

"The book's called *Flowers in the Blood*. I'm almost finished. A bit more research just to check my facts and a little cleaning up. It's about endorphins and how they work on the brain to ease pain. The endorphin receptors and the morphine receptors share common characteristics. This is a new field so it's not something the medical community is completely up on."

Ira was fond of reading medical journals. He had recently decided on his future goal of becoming a doctor. He'd dropped out of high school and hit the road at sixteen, so when he committed to studying medicine around fifteen years later, he started by getting a high-school diploma through the GED Exams, then college classes with prerequisites, a BS, and continued through medical school and internships. A very bright and focused cat, he did this all with sweat and determination. Over twelve years after this conversation, Dr. Jaffe began his career as a surgeon.

"William's been talking about endorphins lately," I told him.

"William's always a few steps ahead of the experts," Ira said. "They get so caught up in detailing that the big picture remains just out of sight until it's in their face. Bill doesn't have that problem."

I went into the archive room to make a phone call. When I returned William was entertaining Jeff and Ira with his recent discovery that a fellow Methadonian on the Karkus program happened to be a famously accomplished New Orleans piano player and a doctor of voodoo. The guy gave William a cassette, which we listened to.

"I don't know much about his music of course. Most of our conversations have been about stool softeners."

After a while we saw that William was winding down. Victor and I cleaned up the table, did the dishes, and policed the area for debris.

I still had no feedback on the pages I had given Howard and William a short while ago, but the story was swelling from a shorty to a possible short novel... It was coming out of me as if by magic.

In June of 1980 Howard Brookner invited me to perform in a scene from *Naked Lunch* titled "The Lavatory Has Been Locked For Six Solid Hours. I Think They're Using It As An Operating Room." It is the only scene in Howard's movie that is staged, rehearsed, acted. In short, not documentary. It is the only scene directly from the novel *Naked Lunch* ever filmed, with Burroughs playing the glorious Doctor Benway. I was cast in the role of Doctor Limpf, Benway's appalled assistant. In the scene, Benway performs a dramatic but unsuccessful emergency heart operation with a toilet plunger. Jackie Curtis, fabulous Warhol superstar and transvestite, plays a pickpocketing nurse.

I arrived at the Bunker on the day of the shooting, a Friday, at 1 pm. Howard was on the phone prepping for combat. His crew was scurrying around the bunker. William waved me into the bedroom. We sat and smoked a fat reefer in seclusion. William wore a white doctor's operating smock and stethoscope, which somehow didn't look all that unnatural on him. We discussed the mounting accumulations of drooling undead outside of CBGB every night until Howard came in and handed me a garment like Doctor Benway's. He adjusted my stethoscope and buttoned the smock up to my neck. "We don't want to get blood all over you."

"Blood, blood for Benway," William muttered.

"Okay, when do we start?" I asked Howard.

"Jackie is getting made up. Lighting and sound setting up. The whole crew is ready. You guys should come out in a few minutes."

When we walked out of the bedroom, the Bunker was jumping with activity. Jackie Curtis was finished with her makeup and trying to decide on a serious matter. Seconds after we were introduced, she wondered aloud, "Should I wear my tits for this scene?"

I wasn't ready to take on such a philosophical question, so I shrugged. "I'm sure you'll know when the moment comes."

Jackie looked at me warmly. "Oh, Dr. Limpf. Is this your debut?"

I confessed to being a touch nervous.

"Oh, you're going to do fine. You inspire such confidence. Are you really a doctor?"

"Yes, but I hate sick people. My practice is focused on cross-species breeding. Can you imagine the offspring of a rhino and a platypus?"

"Wow! How uncommon," she yawned. "Well, just be yourself and it will all work out." Jackie checked herself in the mirror again, pursed her lips, and said, "I don't need these." She put the falsies down and lifted her head high. "I'm woman enough without 'em."

Howard moved us all into the large bunker bathroom, which had urinals and old-fashioned toilet stalls with marble walls and wooden doors. A wooden water box above each toilet featured a pull chain. The lights were bright and hot. Bodies were stuffed into the area near the urinals. A young guy with prematurely graying hair was on sound. Howard introduced him as Jim Jarmusch. The name would not have meant anything to me back then, but I was struck by his air of serene competence.

The patient was laid on a table next to the urinals. One of the film crew then carefully placed a large plate on his chest and spread a huge chunk of uncooked meat on it. Bladders of stage blood were arranged and set to detonate.

Doctor Benway crackled with jubilation as he was assisted into operating gloves. The grand old practitioner of medicine was coming alive inside of him.

We got into position. Howard eyeballed everyone, stepped back, and said, "Action."

My cue kicked in as Benway picked up a toilet plunger and said, "Make an incision Dr. Lymph. I'm going to massage the heart."

I lacerate the guy's chest, cutting into this raw meat. Then I take what looks like insanely large pliers, insert it in the wound, and pull it apart as blood explodes all over us. Then I look at Benway and say, "The incision is ready, Doctor."

Benway and his plunger make a blood-spewing effort on the patient's behalf until Nurse Jackie says, "I think he's gone, Doctor."

"Oh well, all in a day's work. Clean up this mess. I can't be expected to work under such conditions."

The camera then follows Doc Benway to the medicine chest, where he holds up an Rx tube in disgust. "Some drug addicts cut my cocaine with San-EEE-Flush. Nurse, send the boy out to fill this Rx on the double."

Nurse Jackie is thus interrupted from going through the deceased's pockets.

"Cut!"

All in one tape! After the shooting, which

of course ran late, I had to book it over to the office. The accountant was due, and we knew from experience that the guy billed us for every second, even if he sat on his ass smoking a reefer and flirting with staff. I was standing outside the Bunker trying to hail a cab when a very concerned Puerto Rican woman came up to me.

"My God, Doctor! What happened?"

I looked down at myself and realized I was still wearing the white smock covered with stage blood. "Ahm, just a little nosebleed. The patient will probably pull through."

After a few cabs carefully avoided me, I decided to go back upstairs, get rid of the smock, and wash off the blood. Benway was still in costume. Enjoying it a little too much from what I could tell. I pulled myself away and taxied over to the office.

SUNDAY, JUNE 8TH 1980

All my spare time for a full week went to reading Huncke's *Guilty of Everything* manuscript. At the Bunker I told William I liked it and he asked me why.

"It's authentic and perverse," I said. "Pure gold."

"Crude gold," he replied.

"Well it's unselfconscious. Reminds me a bit of Emmett Grogan's *Ringolevio*. Amoral and charming."

"Yes, it's got a raw power. For me Jack Black's

You Can't Win is the apex of that kind of writing."

Dinner guests were due. James came out of the archive room. Victor Bockris showed, then Ted Morgan. We jabbered for a few minutes, then went upstairs to Giorno's loft. John's a great cook. Lobster mousse with steak tartare.

Ted's a French Count turned Yankee Doodle. Years ago he'd written a few novels for New Directions under his French name, Sanche Charles Armand Gabriel de Gramont. As Ted Morgan, he was noted for being a world-class biographer, having published biographies of FDR, Churchill, and Somerset Maugham. Bill once said that Ted's biography of Maugham was more amusing than anything Maugham ever wrote. Ted capped this respectable list of credits with a Pulitzer Prize in journalism. He was worldly and intellectual and well equipped to converse with William on equal footing: a member of the Literary Establishment who truly comprehended William's genius. William was always a little restrained, as if whatever happened around Ted was on the record. I believe he saw Ted as an enlightened ambassador from a world that had long rejected him. Many others in the blue-chip lit cliques still treated him with a mixture of horror and contempt but Ted was completely aware of Burroughs' brilliance. Bill appreciated the flow and polish of Ted's biographies and saw his value as a writer and friend.

Man, these cats could drink. Never saw anything like it. I didn't have so much as a cocktail but almost everyone else was digging hard into the vodka.

William told Ted that Huncke had visited my office and given me his manuscript. He giggled slightly while mentioning the scam Herbert tried to pull with an ounce of grass in his sock.

Ted asked me what I thought of Huncke.

"The criminal mind. Not as evolved as Bill's, of course."

"Is that enough to provoke interest?"

"The guy's got a screw loose but he's irrepressible. Falls on his ass, gets up and dusts off, then right to what he was doing when he fell on his ass."

"He almost walked out with two ounces," William chuckled.

"How's the writing?" Ted asked.

"Well, he's not exactly writing," I said. "He's telling stories, which were tape recorded and typed up, edited. But the voice of Herbert Huncke comes through. Whatever happens, he persists."

Bill shrugged. "Most thieves do. Hey, did you hear about Henry Miller?"

"What? What happened?"

"Gone. He checked out the other day. I heard it on the radio."

I felt a shudder of sadness. Miller's novels had enriched my youth and were in fact the first books I'd read with real interest. I remembered a tattered Evergreen Black Cat edition I'd found in a used bookstore on Flatbush Avenue. Miller's wild adventures made a reader out of me. The Grove Press Black Cat logo became an icon of heroic defiance for me as I knew that whoever was behind that imprint operated fearlessly and in a hostile environment. Kids passed around copies of *Tropic of Cancer* until they decomposed. I went on to suck up the *Rosy Crucifixion* and *Black Spring*. Within a few days of finding that book I began keeping a journal for the first time. I excused myself and went downstairs to catch my breath. I hadn't thought about Henry Miller much in the past few years. But I took some comfort in knowing he was living in Big Sur in a house full of giggly Asian girls with whom he liked to play ping-pong.

A few days later I was getting ready to leave the office William called to let me know he was taking a break from writing and would be reading the story—about thirty pages I was considering as the opening of a novel—in the next few days.

FRIDAY, NOVEMBER 21ST, 1980

Good night at the Bunker with Bill, Herbert, and Louis Cartwright, who took photos. Bill and Huncke slid into old stories, which was extremely entertaining. They focused on Jack Melody and Phil White, who was known as "the Sailor" in *Naked Lunch*. Later I was doing the dishes and Bill held a joint to my lips. He was making us roar with laughter describing the Sailor's habit of falling asleep in the middle of a sentence. Herbert's laugh is wicked, thick, and phlegmy, framed in coughs.

Bill told me he started reading the pages but got distracted by a phone call from Howard; a detail concerning the documentary. He said Howard had mentioned reading my pages and told him I had broken through to a clarity he liked.

We talked about Jack Gelber, who was my playwriting teacher at Brooklyn College. The thirty-page play I gave Bill at City College seven years earlier had been written for Jack's class. A few weeks later Bill told me to throw it in someone else's garbage can and just keep moving forward. I was kind of quiet for a while, which might have prompted William to express frustration. "You are at the cusp of pulling some life out of your characters. What the fuck is holding you back?" That simple question gave me something to think about. His comment was meant to fire me up, not to discourage me. And fire me up it did. I had my characters. I had something to say. I'd continued to show William my writing attempts over the next seven years and in that time he'd prop me up simply by taking my efforts seriously. I was desperately fighting for salvation in my own eyes. He could smell it. He knew.

WEDNESDAY, NOVEMBER 26TH, 1980

Just spoke to Bill and Bockris. Thanksgiving dinner at the Bunker tomorrow at 6 pm. That gives me time to see the folks first. Victor's excited about a five-page piece Bill wrote for *Report from the Bunker*.

THURSDAY, DECEMBER 18TH, 1980

My spirits were lifted. Bill was returning to the City after working on *Place of Dead Roads* in Kansas for a few weeks. I picked him up at Kennedy. He was friendly and warm. Work on the novel had gone well in Kansas and his mood was good.

We scored some chops from a butcher shop on Eighth Street. The butcher asked us to do him a favor and return the bones. Bill got a huge kick out of this. "You think he jerks off with the bones people return? Butchers must be into strange things, hey?"

"He probably has customers who have dogs," I speculated.

Bill laughed. "Of course. Dogs."

We hit the Bunker and while Bill unpacked, I called Victor Bockris and told him to come over as we had more food than the laws of digestion allow.

Bill was still in a smashing mood. The subject of diseases came up and invoked Doctor's Benway. "Things happen quickly, my dear. You go to bed with a little pimple on your dick and wake up in the tertiary stages of syphilis."

Victor brought up a murder case in the news. The Scarsdale Diet Doctor, Hy Tarnower, had been shot and killed by his amphetamine-addicted ex-lover, Jean Harris. Harris was a poised and very classy lady, headmistress of a ritzy girl's boarding school.

"See man, she stepped over the line," Victor said. "You are not supposed to shoot Hy."

"She shouldn't go to jail," I injected. "The guy addicted her to speed, then cut her off. He made her crazy and dumped her."

"Man, these guys make a lot of money and they just start to indulge themselves," Bill said. "He must have had an insatiable pussy habit."

"She is going to jail," I said. "I think her lawyer blew it."

Bill perked up. "Oh man, he totally blew it. Having her show up in court looking classy and aloof. She should have appeared humble, a broken woman, insisting that the awful old cootie forced her to perform feeelllllaatio upon his person. The judge would have pounded his gavel and said, 'Enough! Madam, you can go home. Time served.' Then he'd bus the entire jury over to the cemetery to piss on Hy's grave."

We were laughing so hard it hurt. Suddenly I saw Victor turning white as a ghost, his face blank and eyes swimmy.

"You okay?"

"What? Sure, sure."

He didn't look okay. As Bill got up and walked into the bedroom for some pot, Victor fainted cold. I was standing close enough to break his fall and he wasn't hurt but he didn't seem to be breathing. I pushed on his chest a few times and he exhaled audibly and then caught his breath. I had him lean his head into a cold towel. Minutes later he was disoriented but on his feet.

"What happened, Victor?"

"Listening to Bill, my head started to spin."

Bill had been in the bedroom. He returned to the table with a reefer the size of a cigar.

Victor shook his head. "All that laughing. Guess it got to me."

"So Bill, how was Europe?" I wanted to take the eyeballs off Victor so he could collect himself.

"Great. Stayed with Howard Brookner in Paris. I saw the Benway scene from his film and it's quite good. Doctor Lymph, you are a credit to the medical profession."

I bowed modestly.

"I was paid to be on a panel discussion, and you know how those things go. A fucking windbag festival. But it paid for the trip, and I saw a lot of Brion Gysin, which made it worthwhile. Brion is always onto something. Aside from him not much is happening in the world of painting. It's the same thing over and over. There hasn't been an artistic rut of this caliber since Stonehenge. Say Lymph, what do you make of this condition?" Bill dropped a photo on the table. It was a picture of an African kid completely disfigured by smallpox. "Look at him! Yesterday he was as healthy as you and I. Now he's got a fibrose festering twenty-pound tumor nestled in his left testicle. A big juicy blob that maturated overnight. These things happen you know. Look in the mirror for your morning scrub and there it is! Fat and festering. All you can say is, 'Howdy, big lump.'"

Mr. Bockris took decisive pains not to look at that photo.

"See Lymph, the more spectacular diseases

don't always come to you. You must go out in the field and *find them*! Get your hands dirty! Hump your medical supplies up into the mountains. Shit in the bush and wipe your ass with a hairy muskrat."

I protested. "As a medical man, I cannot endorse the muskrat as a safe butt-wiping tool. The fuckers have teeth and claws."

"Well so do I."

On the day after Christmas 1980 I found myself at the big table in the Bunker with William, Allen Ginsberg, and Peter Orlovsky. I'd given Bill a large stereo cassette radio the day before and Billie Holiday was oozing softly through the smoke-filled hollows.

"See my new radio, Allen. It pulls in alien broadcasts."

"From where, Bill?"

Bill shrugged. "Interzone. There are still Nova criminals out there waiting for their time to come. The right moment! Puff! It's the same pestilence I have been monitoring throughout my career as an agent. They are getting stronger, more complex, and determined. Oh, it also plays cassettes."

"Sounds like the International Jewish Conspiracy."

"No... not entirely."

"Got any Ajax, Bill?" Peter inserted.

Allen smiled indulgently. "It's probably under the sink, Peter. That's where most people keep that sort of—"

"It's in that drawer, Peter." Bill pointed. "Feel free to engage the rags as well."

I'd heard the rumors, so was only mildly shocked as Peter entered into a systematic campaign of buffing and polishing. He soon had the entire dining and kitchen area glowing, and only paused to rest because the fridge had to defrost before he could caress it to purity with his trusty rag.

"Hey Bill, can I go lie down in the archive room?" Peter asked. The second he stopped moving Peter began to decompose.

"Of course, Peter, of course."

As soon as he left the room Allen shrugged. "I know, Bill. What can I do? He has always loved amphetamines. Well, at least you have a sparkling kitchen."

"True... true."

"What's happening with your methadone treatment?"

Bill chuckled. "Nothing's happening. I'm being treated for my addiction and it's working out well. I am, you see, 'a recovering heroin addict being maintained on methadone until my treatment is completed.' I can now operate heavy machinery and play the violin, which I could not do before my first tank of petrol."

"And how about your sex life? Doesn't methadone slow one down?"

"Nonsense, the juice adds octane. Methadone makes you randy as a billygoat! A gelatinous billygoat."

Allen looked at me. "Bill's putting me on. He's been doing that for my entire adult life."

"Well, if you want to know about the combination of sex and methadone, Allen, you *could* dig up somebody who has more to say on the subject."

"Bill has a very shy side," Allen said softly, almost to himself. "It's been a while since I hit the baths. How about you, Bill ol' boy? You getting around a bit?"

"No Al, ol' boy. I have not been to the baths in quite a while. I can do my scrubbings right here in the Bunker."

"Sure Bill. Your scrubbings."

I developed the distinct feeling that Allen was pushing a little too hard. No one ever asked Bill about his current sex life. The man had his dignity, his privacy. I felt as close to William Burroughs as I'd ever felt to any trusted friend, but we were not on farting terms.

I attempted a change of subject. "Allen, tell me about Jacques Stern. I keep hearing these astonishing tales from William."

"Jacques Stern is a man among men," Bill issued flatly. "A veritable warrior of the Dark Regions."

Allen laughed. "A warrior in a wheelchair. Interesting image and oddly correct." He turned to me. "You have met him?"

"No... I await the honor."

"And it is an honor, although a month into his acquaintance you might start wishing you were never born."

William and Allen laughed privately for a moment or two.

"He seems to be one of those reclusive figures, like Harry Smith, who feeds the imaginations of important artists," I ventured.

"Certainly is a factor."

"More than that, Allen," Bill corrected. "More than a mere factor."

"You should meet him, Stew. He's an experience," Allen enthused.

"A man of deep learning and transcendence. Jacques is precisely the type of person a writer should have around him. If, that is, one has a flexible sense of humor and endurance."

"Certainly endurance," Allen added. "But there is a generosity of spirit. A piercing lunatic intelligence."

Peter emerged from the archive room and sat down at the table. Allen poured him a glass of Coke.

"Did you get to rest, Peter?"

"I'm still tired. We should go home now, Allen."

"Yes, it's getting late," Bill agreed. "I have to be at the doctor's office in the morning."

"Where's your doctor, Bill?"

"Why he's in his office, Peter," Bill sang sarcastically. His appointment was with Doc Karkus. Bill did not want people to know every move he made.

Peter looked hurt for a second, then shrugged it off. He'd known Bill Burroughs long enough to sidestep a little crabbing from the man. "Don't forget to wipe off your fridge, Bill. I'm too tired or I'd—"

"Thanks Peter. Don't give it another thought."

I prepared to leave with them. I watched them saying goodbye. Life-long friends hugging each other self-consciously. Intensity and depth marked every gesture and produced a formality tailored to their unique bond. There was a submerged vibe between Allen and William that bordered on impatience. But this shared humor was so refined a part of their relationship it only touched the surface as a faded ghost.

The next day I found myself up at Cousin Sam's co-op perched over Federal Plaza on the downtown end of Mulberry Street. A gathering of the family.

Since our families lived together in East New York Brooklyn when we were kids, and he is eleven years older, I'd often get the kid-brother treatment. Sam was a brilliant student and concert pianist: first of the tribe to attend college and Princeton at that, then to Italy to study music composition on a full scholarship. I used to hide under his piano when the adults erupted. He was a big influence. It was Sam who first triggered my interest in books. I was maybe four or five, leafing through one of his books and complained that there were no pictures. He assured me there were pictures in the book, but you had to make them yourself in your head and the lines of words told you what the pictures looked like. I'd always enjoyed making pictures in my head and was alive with curiosity. That was the first time I found myself wanting to know how to read.

After leaving Sam's I bought Maurice Girodias' biography at Saint Mark's Bookshop.

I had hoped to write at least one strong novel by age thirty-three. My writing life was so often diverted by business it was driving me mad. I sat in the living room nameless and unknown, having made no contributions to American letters. Then there was the marriage breaking up, the dope habit, the risky moves that had me skimming over the surface of a raging stream. I had filled reams of paper without producing anything that was important, that would live.

Something prevented me from penetrating certain areas of my life. Now I felt more vulnerable than ever before. As the night lifted and dawn approached, I sat in the void without armor. The excitement, the schmooz, the reefers, the broken living arrangements, and the fractured sleeping patterns had me in a very vulnerable state. Memory chips passed through my head in a disconnected newsreel. I felt distanced from emotions, free to explore even the most painful fuckups and mistakes. It was all material for a writer: a grim and stabbing entertainment. "It is fear of failure that fuels my nightmares," I said softly. No one heard or answered as I blinked in the new light of day. "Write a few good pages and this cloud will lift," I told myself.

But my writing hand was frozen and I was alone.

SUNDAY DECEMBER 28TH, 1980

Christmas has an impact on the street. A pervading sense of temporary tolerance between dealer and customer, between the junkies and police. I walk these streets with a blade and mace spray but so far luck's been with me. I've seen the car behind me snagged by the law, the guy who'd scored just before me ten minutes ago laying in the street with his pockets inside out.

No doubt this scene is crazy. Today I walked up to a large Rican who was cutting fruit with a long gleaming blade, walked into an abandoned building with him, and scored. Scoring puts you in a strange space. The cops are not there to protect you; they're there to fuck with you. But if they weren't there you'd be in deeper shit because desperation rules these dark conduits. Still, there is some order. The Green Tape crew wears green caps. The Red Line crew wears red bandanas. The bags are sealed and stamped with the crew logo. Perfect for a consumer society. But the quality of these bags is inconsistent, even with the same crew. Red Line can be smokin' in the morning and bullshit in the afternoon. The morning bags spread the word. The afternoon material is mediocre, but people line up for it. Fuckin' bosses must've gone to Harvard Business School. It's the "Vanishing Hotdog." Hotdog gets small, roll gets bigger. The scramblers are working cars and foot traffic and are moving like lightning. They're all packin' blades, some guns, and most of them have been arrested a half dozen times which makes them even more nervous. Even if you're just picking up a lot of things could go bad. Some crews are in hostile competition with each other but can take it out on anyone. "Why're you buyin' from him? Why ain't you buyin' from me?" The scramblers are all spaced out on their own material. To survive they need to be armed. Upper management strut around calm and clean, exempt from the law as they never handle material or weapons. Vendadores do the transactions, and armed guards have their backs.

I called a few friends and told them Huncke would be at the office soon. He'd pick up *New Wave* and read from "Huncke's Journal."

I was sitting in the side room with my partner when Huncke walked in. He was quickly handed a fat reefer and perched in a cushy chair to suck the fumes out of it. He looked at the *New Wave* cover silently, thoughtfully.

"Special Herbert Huncke Issue!" He laughed. "I don't see what's so special about a Herbert Huncke issue, but if that's what you want to call it, fine."

Huncke read my intro in the editorial, which presented a sympathetic and appreciative view of our master of the dark depths. I thought of Huncke as a great liberator and teacher, a wild card with answers to all the wrong questions.

Railriding junkie, jailbird, thief, scam 'n' lam man, 42nd Street stud. Men of his esoterica usually did not write shit down. I stated these factors, shamelessly pumping up the legend of Sir Huncke.

And after he read it twice he looked up and smiled. "I don't know if I'm *all* those things," he said modestly.

"I'm sure your rap sheet would verify."

I was coming to terms with my awakening feelings for Jenny. We'd spoken on the phone a few times since the *New Wave* layout. Long conversations, rich in personal data. I detected more than a casual interest in her tone and was prepared to go out on a limb and confess that she moved me, and I wanted to see her often.

There are moments in life that hit hard and register forever. Split seconds that are just right and never go away. First time I experienced this feeling I'd walked into a corner hangout on Foster Avenue in Flatbush in 1959 and first hearing the Drifters singing "Vaya Con Dios" on the jukebox I thought I was in fuckin' Heaven! I'd had that heightened sense of natural ecstasy only a few times. I can pretend to understand it as an enchantment. Maybe it's as simple as a perfect moment. I'd had that feeling looking at Jenny that day in the coffee shop.

The arrival of the *New Wave* issue gave me an excuse to call Jenny and get together with her. We met on a bench in the east side of the park on Second Avenue and 17th Street. I gave her a few copies of the magazine. We spent a great day together. As these things tend to happen quickly or not at all, we passed a great night together as well. Before long Jenny and her cat Liki moved into my new apartment. We would spend the next twenty-five-plus years together.

I had a business to run, writing to do, and a busy social life inside the Burroughs circle, but I made my own schedule and had plenty of time to hang out with Jenny. We'd meet in the evenings, take long drives on weekends. My view of the world brightened considerably, and I found my interest in heroin diminishing, although not entirely. The schmooz was all around me. Even with Jenny in my life there was no way to escape it.

The manuscript I was working on was progressively gaining substance. I called it *Nightfire* for the evening woodfires burning in oil drums on Houston Street east of Avenue B and on some of the side streets. These blazes serve a dual purpose. They keep the scramblers from freezing and mark a signature of the lotus crews working these dark arteries. Undead can quickly locate and score the stamped glassine dime bags of street dope that distinguish this trade. These fires struck a primal chord I could not locate at first and later realized they brought images of the fires tended by street merchants selling from wooden pushcarts in East New York early and mid-1950s: Pitkin Avenue, maybe Blake Avenue too. These wooden merchants' stands overflowing with fruits, vegetables, fish on blocks of ice, baked goods, large steel scales hovering above, lined the gutters and vibrated with commerce. Fish and produce were more substantial products than the powder-packed glassines with names like Poison, Dr. Cool, Black Sunday, Red Line. But the game was ultimately the same. Donuts to dollars in the brisk air with an oil drum fire to dance around.

One evening I was sitting with Bill at the big table mulling over a writing problem. He had not yet read my pages. I was a little glad. I felt I was on the cusp but not quite hitting it, and considered telling him to hold off until I tightened a few things and could give him a fresher version.

"The manuscript erupts with complications on a regular basis, so that every sitting provokes a deeper frustration. No, there is something missing and I must get it, go there, do that!" I reported.

"Ok, I'll wait to read until you deal with the problem. There are many reasons to get stuck," he warned. "Almost all of them self-generated. As with most problems there is no solution inside the equation. You must go outside."

"Abandon it?"

"Transcend it. When you return to it your critical abilities will have fresh focus. Take the characters into a different space. Walk around with them. See what they are thinking. If they reveal themselves to you, you will be able to contain them on the page... maybe... sort of."

"Oh man!"

"See your job clearly and do it."

"Oh man, you think I'll ever write anything important?"

"Yes, very possibly... because every time I tell you to rip it up and start again, you do. Now don't drag this out. Give me a fresh version within ten days or I'll read the version Howard and I have."

1981

SATURDAY, JANUARY 3ʳᴰ, 1981

"Some wealthy art patrons took John Giorno and I out to a very elegant restaurant last night," he reported. "The food was expensive and awful. People go there to be seen, my dear. Well, the drinks were strong."

"So you wouldn't notice the food was bad?"

Bill laughed. "The problem with rich patrons is they will take an artist out to some terribly expensive restaurant and the first thing they do is make you feel indebted. You would never get to park your ass in such an establishment if it wasn't for them and you should act accordingly."

"What good does that do them?"

"Maybe bring down the price of a painting or a commission." You know, now that we are all chummy we can cut a better deal. Andy Warhol really knows how to play that game. Some patron takes him out to a great restaurant. The waiter comes over. 'And what will you have, Mr.

Warhol?' 'Oh, I'm not really very hungry,' he singsongs. 'Maybe just this glass of water.' Then he whips out a fucking Baby Ruth candy bar and starts slurping on it while the table dips into a bowl of caviar."

"That's brilliant!"

"Indeed. Sends the message that he wants to be *paid* for his art. He will buy his own fucking caviar. And it gives those gold-plated fuckers something to talk about for the next month."

I asked William about the Columbia University scene in the mid-1940s, when he first met Ginsberg, Kerouac, Lucien Carr, and the rest of that circle. The conversation came around to the West End Bar, which is still open and in the same Broadway spot.

"A typical place for students to congregate. Decent food and drinks. Good place to sit and relax. And near the campus."

"I've read about the scene, how everyone met. It's strange how little was said about World War II since it was raging at the time. Did it have much impact on the lives of people around the campus?"

"Oh, of course. The school was full of future military officers taking subjects required for advancement. What were they called...? V-12s, I believe. Everyone read the newspapers. We knew Europe was a mess. The war was a constant presence on the radio and in people's conversations."

"Did people think the States could be the next mess?"

"You mean we might lose? Be taken over by the Nazis and Japanese? That thought was not allowed into the realm of possibility for most Americans. Unless your ass or the ass of someone close was there, the world overseas was a little abstract. But the war had a tremendous impact on life in the States. Civilians' needs were on the back burner. You could not buy a set of tires for your car because all the rubber went to the war effort. Gasoline was rationed anyway so where were you going? On the bright side, you could make a living very easily. Labor shortages saw to that. If you wanted to work, you could find a job without looking too far. With the Great Depression fresh in the public mind, that was no small matter. A wartime economy places the governments involved in a vibrant free-spending mode, particularly when it comes to defense. Government contracts made manufacturers rich and employed an expanded labor pool. Shortages had to be overcome so black markets swelled. Many private fortunes were made during World War II."

"But reading about those years the war is rarely referenced in that circle around Columbia."

"I don't know about that. Everyone had seaman's papers... Allen, Jack."

"Did you?"

"Eventually. Never used them." He chuckled. "Even Huncke managed to do some sea duty. The Merchant Marine paid very well, particularly if you were in a combat zone. Am I missing something? What are you getting at?"

"Okay, what I'm asking is... you guys were living in a world of ideas. Didn't the war short-circuit a lot of that? How can you read the classics while bombs are dropping?"

William laughed. "Bombs are *always* dropping, my dear. There is never a shortage of carnage. Much great literature has been written amidst the chaos of man's capacity to victimize his own species."

"Did you feel compelled to contribute to the war effort?"

"At the time I was having difficulty trying to keep my own balance, let alone the balance of the world. But do not overlook or discount the capacity of literature to impact international situations. Who is more important to the world than writers? You can start or stop a bloody war with The Word."

SUNDAY, JANUARY 4TH, 1981

Quick stop at the Bunker for tea with the old Doc. Now sitting in a coffeeshop prepping papers for the office as the pinkies kick in. Bill gave me a tube of his precious pinkies—tiny codeine tablets—which he picks up whenever in London where they're legally sold over the counter. I'll hold onto the O as long as possible. I can feel the pinkies loosening my bones and told Bill how fragile I was feeling. He said, "Yeah, you got to watch that. Start thinking about a distant relative you never even liked, and you start to boo hoo the poor fucker's dead."

Then we talked about his son's liver transplant and the possibility of ego transplants. I asked him what he thought of Ginsberg's suggestion to apply for writing grants. He shrugged. "Not exactly my specialty but Allen certainly knows all about that."

I began composing a letter to the New York State Council on the Arts for a grant. "Dear Sirs or Madams or Whoever, Mr. Burroughs has just initiated a project that will take time to complete so a young body will be necessary. Perhaps a healthy convict or de-loused vagrant can be provided to... Signed, Allen Ginsberg."

"Yes, yes, we'll send it out at once!"

We talked a bit more about the old days around the West End up near Colombia. Bill looks contrite, tells me the scene where Lucien comes to his door after killing Kammerer, seeking advice. "What if I told him to do nothing— 'Go home and forget about it'—instead of ''Call your family and get a good lawyer, then go turn yourself in.' Sometimes you can see a point in someone's life where a different move would've changed everything."

I said, "He wasn't a real criminal and wouldn't've held up if they sweated him. A lot of people knew they'd been together earlier in the night. Everyone knew the relationship between them. A police investigation was inevitable. Lucien would've gone down anyway and done a lot more than a deuce."

"Yeah, probably."

Then he asked if I was dealing with the

revision of my pages. I told him I'd been slowed down by earthly shit and it was getting on my nerves. This was not quite a complaint. If not for the earthly shit what would I write about? The paradox: that which gives me material locks up large blocks of my time and I need to be in the Void to produce pages.

WEDNESDAY. JANUARY 7TH, 1981

Went to Bill to hear the doctor's opinion on his condition. Before I could ask he said the doc took blood. Results and diagnosis will take a few weeks. Meanwhile he looked chipper. Sneaking vodka and Cokes and blowing reefers. Giorno came down from upstairs and Bill had us cracking with laughter. He didn't have to do much.

He was finally comfortable with the big ghetto-blaster radio cassette deck I bought him. When he first saw it he leaped back as if avoiding a king cobra. "Oh my dear. All those buttons. It's way too complicated for me. Just show me how to turn it on and off." Now he's got it down, listens to tapes of old radio programs and WBAI, etc. James was due in the next day but was postponed. Bill seemed to be riding with it.

Gave one of our typesetters some bucks to pick up bags since he told me he was scoring from the Tuna club. La Tuna bags have a smokin' rep. William wanted a few bags too. Seems they're not pee-testing him much at the Karkus clinic.

Giorno is buddha-goofy in such a great warm

way he is a pleasure to be around. Tired from all-day adventure in bed with "a friend," he looked glazed and spaced. He'd spent the previous evening working on a five-minute poem for the next Giorno Poetry Systems album, which he's now assembling.

On the way back to East 21st Street (almost said "home" but that's not the case) I stopped into 8th Street Books to get a copy of *Evening Sun Turned Crimson* by Huncke—vanity dictates this purchase since a photo of me with Bill, Allen, and Giorno adorns the inner back cover. Also found a copy of Eric Mottram's expanded *Algebra of Need*, English edition. One look at it and I caught the Algebra. Fifteen bucks on books and fifty on dew, not to mention a few taxis and lunch. Got to slow the spending although I'm due bucks from the Litho Company and other less legal sources.

MONDAY JANUARY 13TH, 1981

All set to sleep off the day when Giorno called and asked me to hit the Bunker at 6:30 for dinner.

Bill's busy scrutinizing a first copy of *Cities of the Red Night*. Thrilled to see it in finished form. Bill was a little off. John said it's from a long session working with Bockris followed by a lengthy indulgence last night when Howard showed up with a big piece of coke. With no stabilizing influence in attendance, they fired and banged coke all night.

It's below zero outside. The Bunker's warm

like an oven and the heat on East 21st Street is great but traveling is a test.

Put on Billie Holiday tape for Bill. We smoked a joint and dug the sounds...

WEDNESDAY, JANUARY 14TH, 1981

Bill calls and tells me Maurice Girodias will be at the Bunker later. Too bad I've got to be at the office. Way behind on work and it's got to get done. I waited in the cab while one of our typesetters picked up a bundle of La Tuna, then went to work. The taxi driver was a hip Rican who knew what was going on but chose to talk about the East River and Hudson River freezing. Sat there for ten minutes waiting for the law to descend but they didn't. The guy came back, got in the cab, and we went over to the office.

At 8:00 pm. Bockris calls from the Bunker and tells me to come over and meet Girodias. I appreciate the call but can't cut loose right now. Owning a business is a fuckin' nightmare. Twilight Typesetting allows me to spend much time at the Bunker but there are times I've got to be at the office.

I blew meeting Girodias but he's in NYC lately so I'm sure it'll come up again. Everyone in that literary circle who passes through ends up at the Bunker a few times.

SATURDAY, JANUARY 17TH, 1981

I made it over to the Bunker for dinner with William and Allen. The Bowery was kissed by a chilly wind as I walked downtown from 21st Street. The icy air did not seem to bother the waves of slum bums who spilled from the flop houses and camped—their heads all regal with lush or lotus—upon cold concrete streets.

I'd planned on passing by Dr. Nova on Rivington Street before entering the Bunker but there was a police car outside 7 Rivington and the crew was understandably absent.

I found Allen and William sitting at the big table having cocktails. Allen had brought dinner, and it sat on the kitchen counter still in paper packages from a Chinese restaurant. Allen wanted Bill to hear some Dylan tapes he'd brought over to inaugurate the new stereo, but Bill opted for *The Pan Pipes of Joujouka*, and it was the Pan God who reigned over the hollows. They were in the middle of a conversation.

"I get a shrill potency from him, yes."

"Penetrating, not 'shrill.'"

"Alright, penetrating in a shrill way."

"Maybe to your ear."

"Whose ear would I be hearing him through, Allen?"

I realized they were talking about Bob Dylan. I'd always cherished Dylan's lyrics and delivery. His voice was essential to me at a very young age and had much to do with my desire to write. I had tried a few times to explain why to William. I knew

Allen would be able to articulate Dylan's magic. I'm sure he would have had Bill not changed the subject.

"Huncke's been complaining lately that you don't have time for him, Allen."

"Huncke complaining? I can't imagine."

They shared a chuckle.

Allen went on. "Gregory is the one I'm worried about right now. He's not in great shape. His scene in San Fran is falling apart and he's using a lot of dope."

"I am sick and tired of people thinking that their dope habit is everyone else's problem," William let out. "Gregory is guilty of that and certainly Huncke."

"Huncke is guilty of everything," Allen stated. "Have you seen the manuscript of the same name?"

"He's very coy about showing it to me," Bill reported. "Stew has seen it."

"Yeah, he came up to the office and presented me with a very neat, professionally typed copy."

"How does it read?" Allen asked.

"I like it. It's got that demented magic Huncke does so well. He has a way of making his depravities seem so innocent."

It became clear no one else was going to do it so I laid out plates and set the table. Bill was busy refreshing his vodka and Coke and Allen was attempting to make it through a thick joint of Thai I'd handed him. I was a bit shocked by his determination. I'd seen Allen smoke on many occasions and had observed his policy to be minimal. He would take a few light hits on a joint and pass it quickly. Bill of course would suck the fire from a reefer and toss the charred remnant into an ashtray. But Bill's focus was on booze this evening and Allen's upon the mystic herb.

After dinner Allen pulled out a notebook and read us a few poems. Rhyming couplets metered like sixteen-bar blues. He finished a poem and looked up to get our reactions.

"Alexander Pope? I blurted. I was just goofing of course.

"I wrote that!" Allen snapped.

William laughed and I shrugged. "Relax Allen, he's responding to the structure."

"It's blues structure, not Pope."

"Heroic couplets, Allen. Kind of the same thing."

Allen had a very sensitive and defensive side but I'd never seen it aimed at me before. I almost apologized for the stupid Alexander Pope comment but Allen had moved on so I let it drop.

I was sorry I'd opened my yap. Best to avoid personal conflicts, especially with people I admire. Allen sometimes faced annoyingly negative critique from lesser poets who felt he got too much attention and was sucking up most of the light in poetry circles. He did draw more interest than many, but he was a world-class poet who worked the media skillfully, and often for the benefit of other writers.

I had to remind myself of the essentials. I

was there because I needed to watch William's material go from his head to the page and from draft to draft. Everything else was just a distraction.

"Don't be offended, Allen. Pope was great," Bill said, softening the situation. "I'm sure Stew didn't mean any—"

"I don't even know why I said that, Allen."

"Heroic couplets," Allen said. "William is correct." Allen allowed a slight smile to emerge.

A while later Bill made it clear it was time for him to go to bed. Allen and I left together. The Bowery was frozen, and I moved stiffly opening and re-locking the gate. I looked at Allen, who seemed oddly exempt from the cold, draped in that inebriated Zen calm he had mastered. He was wearing yellow cotton pants and a dark shirt, his jacket bolted shut, face serenely stoned in the iced air.

We walked uptown leaning into the wind.

"Bill seemed a little out of it tonight," Allen noted. "You see a lot of him. Is something wrong?"

"I don't think so. He's working hard on the novel. If it's going well, he feels fine."

Allen nodded. "That's always been true about Bill. Even in the worst of times."

TUESDAY, JANUARY 20ᵀᴴ, 1981

Bill asked if I thought Allen Ginsberg was grouchy the other night. "No," I said. "He was just stoned on very strong pot he wasn't used to."

He then showed off some new weapons from his arsenal and went into a routine about the feasibility of eating rich people if the chips get too far down. "They're fatty. High in carbos maybe but nutritious nonetheless."

The subject of Kerouac appearing on the William Buckley show years ago came up. Bill said, "Jack came off better than Butthead even stone drunk. Buckley's a baboon. If Buckley's upset about something I'm generally glad about it."

THURSDAY, JANUARY 22ND, 1981

Hit the office in the pm just to update the production chart but then put in about six hours on a pulp package for Stosh. Fatigue settled over me and I started making mistakes. Gotta know when to shut it down. I like working in the office when there's nobody around. Maybe someone inputting quietly in the main room but no in and out at night. Easy to get things done.

SATURDAY JANUARY 24TH, 1981

Bill called at 7:30. I was over by 8:00. He wanted to be distracted from an upset stomach and complained about some bad fish he ate yesterday. He didn't want any dinner. I straightened up and made him some tea and an English muffin. No go. Two bites on the muffin and a few sips of tea.

"Oh man I just wanna sleep," said a weary maestro.

I bid adios and flew by Giorno's upstairs. Told him to check on William early tomorrow.

TUESDAY, JANUARY 27TH, 1981

As I entered the Bunker last night Bill jumped up and showed me his new fighting knife and street cane. Like a kid with new toys. Clearly glad to see me. I suspect his good mood is partially due to James being in town. He led me into the bedroom to show off a large picture book with cheesecake shots of glinting fileros.

James was in a great mood too and seemed entirely at home in the Bunker. Always a pleasure to hang with Jazz. He's serious but fun to goof with. An excellent companion.

WEDNESDAY, JANUARY 28TH, 1981

Scored a bundle this morning with one of our typesetters on the third-floor landing of an abandoned building on Sixth Street between B & C. Hair-raising. We're steered in smooth and flying up the stairs and all is well until we get to the landing. I hand the guy a hundred, he gives me one bag and says, "Last bag, now ya gotta wait for the next package." He points to a door and we walk in. The sucker owes me ninety bucks. I'm concerned he'll forget or just disappear. Standing in this wreck of an apartment with a dozen junksick slum bums wishing I was never born. People are sniffling and moaning about the wait. A worker comes to the door. "Ten minutes," he says. The bagman's not around and this guy doesn't know I'm owed nine bags so I can't split. The worker returns in a while and says, "Five more minutes tops."

Eventually I get called. The bagman takes one look at me and gives me a full bundle. "Ya got your play bag," he adds. Before I can leave a cop prowl car shows up outside the building and the guy makes us all go back upstairs and into back into an empty apartment. "Keep down. Stay away from the windows." A blanco lights my cigarette and says, "Probably just be a few minutes. This happened to me yesterday. If there's a prob follow me. I know a way out of this building." He looks me over with a smirk. "You can jump two stories if you gotta, right?"

I pull out my Golden Condor gut and sniff a bag. Now I have patience and big balls. "Sure man, two stories." But the cops leave and we hear "Esta bien" and are ushered out the front door of the building. "Don't run. Take it slow goin' off the block." It's cold out but I don't feel it. Walking casually west feeling the dew creep over me. Ten minutes later I'm smashed and having breakfast at Bini Bon.

Bill: "Never fix in the evening when you don't have to. It only fucks up your morning glory." It's the law of diminishing returns.

FRIDAY, JANUARY 30ᵀᴴ, 1981

The folksies called from nearby so I took them to Fat Tuesdays for brunch. Then they left for Brooklyn and I beat it over to the Bunker. Gave Bill a few bags. James was arranging for them to see him to see people.

Ira Jaffe and Bill were talking at the big table.

Bill and James are going away for a few days and I'll be staying at the Bunker so he showed me where the methadone was stashed and told me I could take a bottle if I needed it.

SATURDAY, JANUARY 31ˢᵀ, 1981

William: "You are here to help descramble the resistance codices."

Yeah, that's the high end. On the bottom I'm ass-deep in the muddy waters of commerce. Running the typesetting shit, the boo which leads me into rooms full of wop and cocky mocky merchants and thieves. I recover in the company of wizards but I'm often left licking my wounds in the dark. Thirty-three and taking pleasure and punches at a frantic pace. I wonder if everyone who owns a legal business breaks the law just to stay afloat. That certainly has been my experience. You're facing a weekly payroll, monthly supply and rent bills, slowly paying accounts payable.

Chalk of boyhood on the factory wall. The young disruptive begins with where he is not going: military, school, factory. All designed to obliterate the Imagination, which is the primary birthright and he who fucks with it is the enemy. The cool voices of outlaws past whispering in the winds. Learning is unavoidable unless you pay attention. The conscious mind dismisses data that sparks no interest. The subconscious takes in every fuckin' thing: advertising jingles, songs you don't even know you know. Harmony is a pleasant interlude but it is discord that will get you respect from the Sirens. Armed but vulnerable, eyes scan for the menace.

It's 1:30 am. I was supposed to go see Wilson Pickett at Privates on 85th Street with James at 1:00 am. but it's cold out and I've got shit to do tomorrow. Spoke briefly to a slurringly inebriated Mr. Burroughs and wished him a safe and enjoyable reading tour—he'll be away on his birthday. I will be taking care of the Bunker. Allen Ginsberg and Peter Orlovsky will be staying there as their pad is full of guests but Bill says, "That shouldn't interfere with you coming and going as you please." He will call with airport info for his return so I can pick him up.

TUESDAY, MARCH 3RD, 1981

The phone rang and it was James.

"Sad news, Stew. William's son Billy died. Come by the Bunker tomorrow. Bill will appreciate it."

I wasn't shocked. This had been coming for some time. I wondered how William was handling it.

Next day I fell by the Bunker. William was melancholy but not distant. He made some tea. We sat at the big table. I cut into a piece of opium. Bill swallowed a full gram. I did a mere quarter gram. Felt it too. James was in and out. Other people were about but we remained alone at the table.

"Why am I surprised?" William whispered. "We all knew..."

"You really did your best for him, William. Seeing it coming is one thing. When it happens is something else. You've got people who care about you. You've got work to do."

"The work is the important thing." Bill cleared his throat. "I'm supposed to be writing an introduction to Jeff Goldberg's book. Haven't felt much like working on it but I really should."

"It will help to get in motion."

"Yes, of course. We are not going to cancel the reading tour. I need to keep going."

There was a weighted sadness emitting from William. I decided to get out of the way. I told him I'd been on silent standby and if he needed anything let me know.

Later that evening Herbert Huncke fell by the new crib on 22nd Street. Leslie had moved out and I took over the rent. The ex-wife planned on leaving the 21st Place and I would have it back, but not for six months or so. Herbert wanted me to meet a friend of his, a Puerto Rican named Valentino who ran a pot crew out on East 28th Street just west of

Second Avenue. "You will like this guy, Stew. He's the mayor of the block... or at least the most reliable employer."

Maybe a week later I got a call from Bill. The first part of the tour was done, and he was in New York for a few days before embarking on the second part. He invited me over for dinner. It was good to see everyone. Howard, James, Giorno. Bill appeared in reasonable spirits although every now and again he'd drift off inside himself. We fucked around with the blowgun for a while.

"After this tour I want to cloister myself away for three months and get a grip on *Place of Dead Roads*," he said. He brought up a few bad reviews of *Cities of the Red Night*. "These so-called critics aren't worth their weight in ruptured condoms. A critic is given a book to read and review. If he doesn't understand it, he decides it's vile. These nameless assholes are prepared to take a man's life's work and piss on it because they didn't get it. They don't like what the writer is saying, and so disregard the one important question: Did the author do what he intended and do it well? A reviewer should refuse to work on a book he has no affinity for or understanding of. 'Give this book to someone who has the background for it. Instead, they take it home and read it, resenting the time they put into earning a lousy hundred bucks for the job."

"Not everyone believes the critics," I said. "There's still word-of-mouth, whispering vines, pockets of independent thought."

"Of course, but the critics can make or break you on the bookstore racks. The people who place orders for the big stores, they don't have time to read books. They read reviews. It can be a disaster. You know Ezra Pound refused to critique novels. His reasoning was since he never wrote a great novel, he had no firm understanding of what it means to write one. He could only tell if he liked or disliked a novel."

"Isn't Pound known for astute criticism?"

"Yes, yes, of poetry. He championed Robert Frost, Joyce, William Carlos Williams. He fucking carved ten pages of gold and removed ninety pages of dross to construct Eliot's 'The Waste Land.' See man, he was qualified to critique poetry because he was a great poet."

"I find it really hard to read Pound," I said. "I've tried 'The Cantos' a few times."

"Heavily coded material. He was writing things only a handful of people were qualified to read. You start referencing from the full spectrum of world literature... it's like shooting holes in the page for the average reader. Joyce did a similar thing although not as shamelessly. Fortunately, the two of them were oddly exempt from a torrent of printed reprimands. You see, many critics were intimidated. They were simply embarrassed to admit that they didn't get it. Of course, there were sections in both of their works that were superb and accessible."

The next day William split for the second part of his reading tour. Things might have calmed down, but as fate would have it one very inebriated Herbert Huncke flopped by 22nd Street. He sat down and we blew a reefer. I watched as he melted into the chair.

"We must walk over to 28th Street, Stew. Valentino is expecting us. I told him you get good moota and he wants to see."

"You don't look like you could walk anywhere."

Herbert produced a paper of cocaine and gunned some powder up his nostrils. The eyes popped wide and he smiled. "Ready?"

I took a pound with me. This was a new thing and I was bringing the man a sample to see what quality he worked with. He'd told me he paid two hundred buck a pound usually, so the sample was appropriate to that figure.

We walked Second Avenue over to East 28th and turned west. Maybe five stores off the corner there was a Latino storefront numbers hole (a betting parlor where people played the horses). I'd passed it numerous times. I knew there was a betting scene but wasn't particularly interested. People selling nickels of moota openly on that block also didn't concern me. I never bought nickels of pot on the street and I never gambled.

We walked directly into the numbers hole, pausing as Huncke and the door guard acknowledged each other. There were several Puerto Ricans sitting around. Older folks playing dominoes, drinking beer, and eating rice, chicken, and beans off paper plates. Racing results came through the radio and television sets. A guy with a broad black mustache greeted Huncke with a snarly smile and eyed me coldly.

"This is the guy I wanted Valentino to meet," Huncke informed.

The mustache nodded silently. He gestured for us to wait, then disappeared. He returned and escorted us into a small rear room, in which a man was fitting a piece of cheesecloth over the mouth of an empty glass milk bottle. The glass was steaming and had obviously been filled with hot water.

"Ah, Valentino, this is the man I was telling you about," Huncke opened. "Specs, meet Valentino. Valentino, Specs."

Valentino was a stocky substantial-looking Rican with curly graying hair and a wide smile. He looked to be in his mid-fifties, muscled, streetwise, direct. A wooden handled .38 revolver was tucked into his belt. Firm eye contact as he shook my hand and invited us to sit down.

"You ok with Mr. Huncke so you ok with me. I need good pot. People out here sellin' good shit. I need better. You get good pot? Give good price I re-up like mad. No consi. No consi. Cash on the drop. I go through a pound or two every day."

I took out the sample and handed it to him, expecting him to scrutinize it immediately. Instead, he placed it on a table and continued what he had been doing as we walked in. He filled a cheesecloth sack with Bustello coffee and dropped a piece of eggshell on top. He positioned the cloth around the mouth of the milk bottle and dripped boiling water through it. I noticed a blob of dissolving sugar on the bottom of the bottle. Then he poured steaming milk into three paper cups and filled the cups with coffee.

"This is very good," I let out.

"Valentino is known for his coffee," Huncke informed.

"Naww man, I'm known for my moota."

We laughed. There was a good feeling at the table and I looked at Huncke with a deepening admiration. I knew how these things worked. When you are invited into a situation on the street, the status of the guy who brought you in determines your immediate standing. I was also impressed that Huncke had used my street name not my real name, without being briefed.

We sat around drinking coffee and learning to relax around each other. He told us his elderly mother was in from Puerto Rico and he was showing her around the city. They'd gone to the top of the Empire State Building and she'd been so overwhelmed by the sight of Manhattan that she burst into tears. He wanted her to move to New York but she refused to leave her chickens and fruit trees.

Maybe a half hour after we walked in, Valentino got around to checking out my smoke. He opened the bag, took a deep sniff, then rolled a few buds between his fingers and smelled his fingers. "Smell like pooosy."

"Earthy puss-puss on a humid day," I added.

He rolled a slender joint, lit it, inhaled deeply a few times. "How much this pot?"

"Two hundred. I can get primo but the numbers go up. This is a strong commercial at a good price."

Valentino called for the mustachio to join us and he promptly did. Mustachio examined a few buds, noting the texture and smell. Then he rolled a reefer and smoked slowly, thoughtfully, appraising the product with much more scrutiny than his boss had.

I knew at once that Mustachio functioned as Valentino's grader. I saw how he slowed down and paid attention to the key details. The smell unlit, the smell and taste lit, the formation of resin on the mouthpiece of the reefer. "Gonna call this a 'regular' or even 'fine regular.' Nice taste. Feel it on the exhale," Mustachio let out with a dense stream of smoke.

Valentino was satisfied. He turned to me. "You bring me two pounds?"

I laughed and pointed to the sample. "One full pound," I said. "I'll bring you another tomorrow."

"Make it two."

Valentino took the pound and went into another room. He came back and handed me two hundred bucks a moment later. Then he said something to Mustachio in Spanish. The man nodded and walked into the front room, returning a few minutes later with three plates of chicken, rice, beans.

Next day Herbert and I walked back to 28th Street with two more pounds. Mustachio—I later learned his name was Israel—ushered me in with a smile. That told me people were liking the product.

Valentino counted four hundred bucks, most of it in fives and tens, and took possession of the two pounds. He told me to drop in on him in a few days.

We walked out and back to my crib. I gave Huncke an ounce of pot and twenty bucks for the introduction. I was paying maybe a hundred a pound so it was not exactly a big payday but surely worth the effort.

"Well done, Herbert. Well done."

"Just payin' you back for all the good smoke you've laid on me."

We sat smoking calmly in the late afternoon air. I asked him if he thought there was any way to help his old friend Bill through the loss of Bill Junior.

"Your impulse to stay out of the way was correct," Huncke said.

"What was William's relationship to his son like in New Waverly?"

Huncke appeared reflective. "Well, Billy was just a tot. William was very absorbed in his own problems. Keeping a supply of opiates going, scoring benny sniffers for Joan who was hooked on amphetamine. Stocking the kitchen. Bottles of liquor disappeared quickly. The house needed constant attention. Repair a fence, fix a leak in the roof."

"Was he good at that?"

"He was not entirely useless." Herbert

laughed. "He could handle rudimentary things but not very gracefully. I was summoned to help around the place. Also to score. I located a drug store that would sell me Benzedrine inhalers by the box and for just slightly over the usual price. Finding pot wasn't much of a challenge either. Texas always had its share of available marijuana. You hook up with a Mexican or a local black cat and you can get all the pot you want. Opiates were another matter. The pharmacies were uptight about dispensing goodies but we found ways to score. Some places they'd make you sign a book if you wanted codeine or laudanum or anything stronger. Some places didn't bother. And Bill had a friend in New York who would mail him grams and quarter ounces of heroin occasionally. So his attention was taken up with these matters. The kids, little Julie and Billy, they were sort of Joan's project. William was certainly indulgent with them, but he did little in the way of caring for them."

"Did William do any writing in New Waverly?"

"Reading, not writing. Not that I knew about. If so, it wasn't his focus. I never saw him writing or heard him talk about writing. That came later."

"Could you tell there was a great writer living inside him?"

Huncke laughed. "Well, Bill was always able to express himself with clarity and distinction. He had a way of cutting through to the heart of the matter instantly when a subject comes up. He was good at locating the important question. I'd always saw that in him, way before he became the version of himself he would later present to the world."

Before Huncke left for his crib in Brooklyn Heights I wanted to know more about Valentino, so I walked him downtown to the subway.

"Well, you see what's going on around the numbers hole. There are four or five people dealing nickels on that block, all for Valentino. They stash product and bank in the numbers hole which is run by an old guy from Valentino's village in the Old Country. Izzy runs the little crew for him. Izzy's the Mustache. The little chubby guy with tattoos you maybe didn't even notice is Coochie. He's always around to cover their backs. There are a few Spanish girls who make up the nickels in a tenement crib down the street. The nickels all have that distinct roll. Valentino calls them barrels because they are rolled in those small manila envelopes. Izzy feeds the crew pot and collects money."

"He must be makin' some bank."

"Oh man, Valentino's supporting a lot of people. Everyone who works for him makes money. And he takes care of his mother, his girlfriend, a bunch of kids. He's got a house in Puerto Rico. If you find yourself doing business with Izzy it's because Valentino's in PR relaxing. He seemed to like you."

"He trusts you so he trusted me. I will check him out in a few days."

"You should. He moves a lot of nickels, man. He will buy from you often." Huncke bid adios and disappeared into the subway system.

*

A few weeks later Huncke dropped in to see how I was doing and pick up some pot. He caught me as I was making up a few pounds for Valentino. He also caught me fighting off a light yen. Ever helpful, Huncke dribbled out a few drops of his thick potent methadone into a glass. A hundred milligrams makes for a very concentrated brew as they use the same bottle—and volume of water—no matter what the dose. I blended in an inch of fruit juice and tossed it down. It would take a while to hit but just knowing it was coming lightened my spirits.

"I've got to go over to 28th Street, Herbert. Wanna take a walk?"

"Certainly. I'll say hello to Valentino."

As we turned off Second Avenue we hit a wall of blue. There were uniformed police all over the street, dashing around their blinking cruisers. The air was dominated by cop radio chirps and static. Fragmented and urgent messages rang through circuits.

"Oh man what the fuck?!?"

"Whatever it is, it's down the block, Stew. Nothing to do with the numbers hole."

"Yeah but... let's not go in. Keep walking."

Huncke smirked. "For God's sake give me the package." He took the wrapped pounds out of my hand and marched into the numbers hole. The uniforms around us paid no attention as I followed him in, more than slightly amazed by his instincts in the field.

The numbers hole was going full blast without a thought to the cop chaos outside. Izzy told us that there had been a stabbing during a domestic squabble up the block. It had nothing to do with pot selling although he did call in his workers. A half dozen of them were lounging around jabbering, waiting for the cops to leave.

"Is bad for business, this stabbing shit," Valentino announced. He stood by the window, arms folded across his chest, frowning out an atmosphere of propriety and disapproval. "Ahh well, let's go in the back. I drip some coffee."

Later I walked with Huncke down Second Avenue. Tired. Having cash in my pocket from Valentino made me wonder what bags were smokin' in the Alphabet. But I distracted myself by making a quick impulse decision to stroll over to the butcher shop on Second Ave near Saint Marks Place and pick up a few lamb chops for dinner.

1982

MAY 24TH, 1982

William was spending most of his time in Lawrence, Kansas. He and James did not want to lose the Bunker so I took over the rent. That way William could use his bedroom when he came to New York to do business or see his friends. Jenny's mother moved into the 21st Street apartment since the ex-wife has moved on. I kept Leslie's place as the rent had been paid in advance every three months. I installed a painter friend who was trying to interest an art gallery in his work and needed to be in New York. All this shifting ended with Jenny and I living in the bunker.

    I was scoring regularly from Dr. Nova just across Bowery on Rivington Street. Whenever I turn off Bowery onto Riv I look for the guy in the broad cap who sits on a folding chair outside 7 Riv. If he's there the crew is working. When Nova sells out BT 82 opens. It's not quite as good but is available until 6 pm. The police totally ignore Rivington Street, passing by on Bowery or Chrystie Street but never turning onto Riv. Makes me wonder how much the crew bosses pay for this arrangement. Manhattan South occasionally bum rushes the crews and makes arrests but not often. They only bust scramblers because the street bosses don't touch product. Within a few hours or days, everyone's back on the street scrambling.

Jenny's brother Bobby stayed over last night. Howard came by early afternoon, excited about the new xerox shop he'd opened in the ground-floor store of the Chelsea Hotel where he and Brad are living. Often Howard comes over early and we meet for Breakfast at Moishe's, last of the old Lower East Side Jewish diners. Then we walk over to Eldridge Street and Houston to score on one of the Newyorican social clubs. I had to pick up a few pounds of bush and drop them off on the Upper West Side. Bobby drives me in his old rust bucket.

Long talk with William on the phone. He was making progress with *Place of Dead Roads* and was under money pressure to get it finished. A few hours later James calls. He and Bill had thought it over and would like me to come to Kansas and type *Dead Roads* from William's typewriter draft into a computer document so it can be edited. My typing speed is legendary and I know what a Burroughs page should read like. The idea of hands-on experiencing a master writer go draft to draft excited me and I agreed, but I wondered how I'd pull off the finances as William wouldn't have his advance from the publisher until the novel was handed in. I figured I'd need about five thousand bucks and went to bed that night wondering how I could pull it off.

The next morning unrelated events broke the mystery. An ex-associate of mine was under investigation for bringing a multi-ton load of pot into New York. He'd made a one-time investment in my typesetting company early in the game, before I had a partner and a solid customer base. He was sure the Feds would be looking to question me about him, since they knew he was among a small group who had helped me launch my typesetting business. He wondered if I'd mind leaving the city for a few months until his lawyers figured out how big a check he'd be writing to the US Treasury to bring an end to the investigation. He said he'd give me five grand to get by on for a few months if I'd agree to this. Amazing timing! Five thousand bucks in crisp aces appeared. A coincidence? The word is without a specific referent. A good example of William's Magical Universe. If you are where you are supposed to be, doing what you are supposed to do, things will fall into place.

After scoring and getting straight I picked up the *Yellow Pages* and located an auto transport company. I arrived at the offices with the required paperwork: driver's license, proof of employment, apartment lease. I was handed the keys to a two-year-old Buick, a transport agreement to deliver the car to an address in Kansas City, Kansas, and two hundred bucks for gas and oil. I called James with the news. I told Jenny to pack. We would be leaving NYC in two days.

That afternoon Herbert Huncke dropped by the Bunker. We were a bit frantic from getting ready to leave the city but it was nice to be distracted for an hour or so. I made coffee. Howard dropped in and we got high. As we were kicking back there was a knock on the door. I was expecting this. It was the five grand from my associate. I opened the door on a familiar face. One of his workers. The guy came in, sat down, pulled his pants down a bit, and pulled out an envelope that had been taped to his leg. He handed it to me and said, "Five K, Specs. Count it."

I quickly verified the count, thanked the guy, and showed him to the door.

"I think Herbert's gonna have a fit if you don't give him a few bucks, Stew," Howard whispered.

I was aware of Herbert's big eye as I tallied the cake. Counting other people's money was an old habit. Most of it was in aces but a few in twenties. I threw him two and said, "This must last for the entire trip and maybe longer, until Bill gets his advance. And I must pay off a friend who loaned me cash a few weeks ago."

Huncke did not look satisfied but my tone was final. On a hunch I might feel bad about not giving him more dough, he asked if he could have the key to the Bunker and use it while we were away. I said, "Of course, but I must ask William. If he signs off on it, yeah."

He said, "Better if he didn't know."

"Even better if we don't betray a friend's trust."

He pocketed the two twenties, finished his coffee, and split.

Over the next few days we visited my parents in Brooklyn and saw Jenny's mother, then gathered the necessary items including enough heroin to make the trip and an Rx of codeine to taper off once we got to Lawrence. Jenny had a mild chippy but I had a long-established habit. I was hoping William kept a stash of methadone as he'd transferred from the up-tempo celebrity methadone doctor that Ira Jaffe had arranged in Manhattan to a clinic in Kansas City. I knew he was getting take-home doses and his nature was to accumulate as much as he could by underdosing slightly. It was what poet and storyteller Marty Matz used to call "the Dreaded Underdose!" Ten or fifteen milligrams from a daily 60 milligram dose and you hardly feel the difference while watching your stash grow.

I knew Howard would watch over the Bunker. He had the key because he was fine-tuning his documentary film on William and the footage he'd already filmed was in the archive room. Howard would take part of it to a loft on the West Side where he could use a specialized machine to cut and splice. Editing was a major part of the process. His film would win in the documentary category at the NY Film Festival in 1984, the same year Grove Press published my novel, *The Lotus Crew*. But we didn't know that in the early summer of 1982 of course. We were just a couple of young junkies wondering what fate was going to throw at us next.

The following morning Howard came by for one last Moishie breakfast. We scored and went back to the bunker to get high. I'd given Howard another thirty pages of *Nightfire* a while ago and he'd had a chance to read it. He was more emphatic than I'd expected. "Has William seen those pages?"

"William has the first thirty pages. Has not said anything yet."

"It's caught a strong realism. If you keep the intensity I think you have something."

I thanked Howard for boosting my confidence. We packed clothes and gear and finally Jenny's cat Liki into the car, said goodbye to Howard, and took off for Lawrence.

JUNE 1982

After three long days on the road we rolled across a narrow bridge and into the little college town of Lawrence tired from the drive, the cat puking in the back, and feeling more than a touch of yen. It seemed like a great idea to only bring a few bundles of dope and some codeine along. Sure, we'll just taper off in Kansas... But the further away we got from New York's open heroin scene the dumber that thinking seemed. By the grace of the Great Demon Humwawa, James and William had anticipated our landing would be less than easy. James handed me a bottle of William's methadone. Sixty milligrams!

"So settle in," James suggested. He and his boyfriend Ira Silverberg had a comfy pad just off KU campus. "Bill is excited about you getting to work so we'll fall by the office after breakfast tomorrow and set you up at a workstation. In the evening we can ride out to the stone house to see Bill. A friend of Ira's knows a student who's giving up an apartment a few blocks from the office. You can check it out when you have time."

James' office was in the Masonic Hall building. Above the hall was a rather formal office building. Windows looked out on Mass Ave, the main street of town. He had a good computer and a comfortable chair. I sat and looked over the manuscript for an hour. It was readable but not without problems. William had switched typewriters repeatedly, manual to electric and back to manual, ribbons getting worn making for light spots. Flipping around I noted a few portfolio irregularities. These are the kind of things that slow down a job, so I decided to allow an hour before each session to familiarize myself with the day's pages. Jenny helped me with this to speed it up. I knew they were having cash-flow problems and a nice check was to be drawn upon handing the novel to the publisher, so this challenge was not without pressure.

Later that day we dropped the transport car off in Kansas City and returned to Lawrence in a cab. James took us to a car rental place where we picked up a little Japanese car for getting around while we were in Kansas. I could have walked to the office but no one in Lawrence walked anywhere and William's stone house was a few miles into the countryside so a car was necessary.

The next day I got to the office early and put in my first full session. I scraped a light hit of speed off a gram chunk into a cup of coffee. I managed a full day's work and piled up twenty-five pages. Jenny went over the first twenty as I polished off the last five. I'd been too focused on speed and accuracy to dwell on content and only later realized the magic I'd been feeling as William's magical writing passed through me and into the document.

James told us William wanted us to visit for dinner. He planned on joining us but had some music business to take care of so suggested we stop for take-out from a local fried chicken joint Bill liked. They also sold corn and other vegetables.

As we were getting ready to drive to the stone house, James placed a long-barrel Colt .45 on the dashboard of the car. I was a bit shocked. "Guns don't get a second glance out here, Stew. William asked me to have you bring this along." He handed me detailed directions to the stone house. "Don't smoke pot in the car. If you get stopped, guns are fine, but guns and pot will earn you some scrutiny."

It was late afternoon when we turned into the driveway of William's rented house, a structure of old-fashioned well-fitted stone masonry. Bill was on the back patio. He rose and greeted us warmly. We settled in as he went inside to put down the food we'd brought and make tea. A few minutes later we were being shown the old barn where he set up his paintings. He would place a canvas against a far wall, step back twenty or so feet, and shoot the painting with his shotgun or .38 revolver. A few paintings were drying against an inner wall. "Well, let's smoke a joint and have some tea before dinner."

Jenny lingered in the barn a few minutes while Bill and I smoked. Her Art History background engaged as she took in the workings of Bill's creative output.

As we sipped tea and relaxed, a snow-white cat with crossed blue eyes appeared and stood before Bill impatiently.

"Somebody's making demands," Jenny said.

"Indeed, and his four hungry beggar associates are not far behind," William guessed.

A second later four more cats appeared, all of them focused on every move William made.

"I will get no peace until I deal with this," he sighed, using his arms to propel himself out of his chair.

"Are they all yours?" Jenny wondered. She was so delighted she'd broken her cautious silence around Bill.

"They certainly seem to think so. This started with Whitey. He just appeared one day and went to work on me until I fed him. Next day he was back with his posse."

"Wow! What adorable little creatures!!"

"Oh, they've all been to charm school,"

William muttered, adding what a pain in the ass they'd become as he popped open cans with a flourish and laid out a line of plates. Whitey and his posse were skiting about impatiently waiting for the erect vertebrae to get out of the way so they could get down to business. And before long we did the same. Vegetarian Jenny had a baked potato and corn. Bill and I went for the chicken. After dinner we blew some local pot and kicked back. William was very pleased we'd signed on for the long journey and job ahead. He wanted the novel in his agent's hands as quickly as possible. I assured him it was an honor to be trusted with his manuscript and I understood time was a factor. I explained how I worked: two- to three-hour sittings, twice a day. Each session should produce fifteen pages. I would take a quick scan to familiarize myself with the pages I had to cover before typing. Jenny would read as I typed to spot any overt errors or problems that may result from the rapidity I would need to meet my daily quota. She would also review the day's pages and list any questionable details.

"How long do you think it'll take you?"

"I'm hoping four weeks will do it. I'll be able to give you a better estimate after I get a full week into it."

EARLY JULY 1982

I hit the keyboard right after breakfast. The workstation was comfortable. Two hits on a reefer and I went to work. I did a solid two hours before my typing slowed down. Jenny came by and we had lunch, then took a short walk across the nearby train yard, the river, back to the office. Refreshed, I hit it for a full three hours before my typing slowed down and I started making mistakes. I've learned not to push beyond that point because it can be counterproductive: you overdo it one day and might have trouble starting the next. Pacing is vital. Keyboard is mostly muscle memory. There's no thinking involved: mental focus should be on the content of what you're typing, not the physical act. I had my twenty-five pages and was enjoying the novel's flow. Jenny became fascinated by William's writing style. She was a compulsive reader, well read and fluent in Farsi and Hebrew as well as English. Farsi would one day lead her into a deep study of Sanskrit. While editing my emerging novel as well as pulp writing, her natural editing skills tightened. She was never formally taught to edit but found herself naturally able. She was moved by the architecture of verbal and written communication. William's experimental playfulness triggered her interest and caused her to examine how he was achieving such striking results.

Over the following days I did little but work and sleep. Jenny had found a bike for sale which launched her on a solo exploration of the town. I was making great time and had fallen into the spell of William's ever-brilliant writing. It fascinates me how a master stylist tosses images at the reader. I was typing the Burroughs of *Cities*, not of *Naked Lunch* and the cut-up trilogy. This

Burroughs was less familiar to me: an evolved genius. I missed "ol' Whispering Lou down at the fillin' station" and "Limestone John and Hamburger Mary," but this was a new time and space. The earlier work was non-linear and textured with vivid vertical sparks. The story emerged more through an accumulation of details—often presented as presuppositions—than a fixed structure. Personnel popped in and out, often in the same paragraph. A routine might open with a bang and run for a dozen pages, every sentence a jewel. What I was typing now was more formally structured, less volatile, yet sacrificed none of the distinctly articulated music of Bill's Burroughs' magical word play. Days melted together and the computer manuscript grew. I was completely engaged with the task and what happened around me became vague. I do recall Allen Ginsberg arrived a few days before July 4th.

JULY 4TH, 1982

We attended a barbecue at James' friend Wayne's house just across the Bridge. From his backyard you could see the train tracks and his neat vegetable garden. Allen, Peter, and Bill were the guests of honor and the locals—many of them James' friends from college—were pleased to be in their company. At some point Peter invited Jenny to explore the garden. He was dizzy with the delight of pulling carrots out of the soil and munching on them. Jenny found this charming.

That night I told William the manuscript was

completely input in document form, ready for editing. I saw his spirit lift. It had taken much time and energy for him to get the novel assembled enough to accomplish this vital step. He had work ahead of him but James was standing by and at long last there was an end in sight.

A few people were sniffing cocaine but William stuck with his vodka tonic. After a while he asked if I'd drive him back to the stone house, so we got in the car and drove off as the sun went down. I hadn't driven around much at night and it got very dark quickly. New York City never got nearly this dark. It was a bit of a challenge but soon we pulled into the driveway. Jenny suggested we walk William to the door, as he had been drinking heavily and visibility was limited. As we made it from car to his door the sky cracked open with bolts of brilliant lightning. For a split second it was light as day, then back to inky blue blackness... then another loud crackle and a second of daylight.

"What the fuck?" I let out.

William laughed. "An electric storm is all. Happens all the time."

"Not in New York," I let out in amazement.

MID-JULY 1982

We rolled into the Lower East Side on a dark summer night, then quickly unloaded the car by the Bunker, settled in, and put on coffee. I knew we wouldn't sleep. We both had the same thought: I would be out at daybreak picking up some dope. Our habits were light at the time because William's stash of excess methadone had been hit hard during our tenure in Kansas. I was down to under ten milligrams a day and Jenny maybe half of that. But rolling through the streets of the Lower East Side had us itching to score. We wanted to wash all that wholesome bright Kansas sunshine out of our bones and get good and smashed. And we knew it would take very little dope to get nice.

It was a bit of a shock to turn onto Rivington Street and not see the guy with the newsboy cap sitting outside 7 Riv. There were a few familiar faces outside the bodega next door but no one was touting Dr. Nova. Since I was a familiar customer I was told Rivington and Bowery was shut down by the cops. I could pick up a block east in the strip of park that runs along Chrystie Street. If they weren't there I had to go to Eighth street and Avenue D. Shit, things change quickly on the street but I wasn't junksick and saw this as a minor annoyance. I started walking east. The strip of park was infested with police so I continued through it and made my way onto Allen Street. Cop cars prowled slowly through the old narrow street until Avenue B where the police presence magically lightened. I turned north at Avenue D and made my way up to Eighth Street, where I heard the touters loud and clear. This was open turf shared by a few crews. I saw a black girl called Starlight who often told me what bag was smokin' now and waved to her. She approached.

"Hey Specs, where you been?"

"Outta town. What's going on here?"

"Dr. Nova not out yet today. They open around noon and stay open late. Cops got a hard-on for Nova. The 'Green Tape Lovers' is on the money. Things have changed. Come with me."

Starlight led me to a doorway where she introduced me to a Latino guy she called Rene and assured him I was ok. Rene sold me two bundles and smiled when Starlight reminded him to include the "play bags." Rene handed me two extra bags as I gave him four fifties. I gave Starlight the play bags for telling Rene that I was ok to do business with. Starlight was very happy with this. I really liked her. You could tell she'd been very pretty when she first hit the streets as a fresh young hooker. Ten years shooting dope and coke had taken the bounce out of her step but she was honest and always pointed me to the smokin' bag of the moment. I often laid a half ounce of pot on her when I needed all my cash for bags of dope.

"So if you wanna score early tomorrow go for the 'Black Sunday' at Chrystie Street and Rivington. They open at 7:30. Dr. Nova also works there but doesn't open till noon."

"Thanks Star."

I walked back to the Bunker cautiously. Every few blocks there was a police car rolling at a hostile crawl. I saw a guy from the BT 82 crew and nodded hello. He approached.

"Stay away from Riv off Bowery. Manhattan South making crazy busts on that block. Most of my crew got busted and word is they will be busted again on sight."

"Sorry to hear that."

The BT 82 crew was Dominican, not Puerto Rican. I wondered if that had anything to do with it. I soon learned there were a few new Dominican crews working Alphabet City.

I continued back to the Bowery. As I was crossing Stanton and Chrystie Streets, I saw Gregory Corso get out of a car with Jersey plates and walk towards Riv. I noticed there was a girl at the wheel. I'd heard from William that Corso was back in the City and had a girlfriend in New Jersey who was taking care of him. I stopped him and told him to go to Eighth Street and Avenue D."

"Fuck," he let out, turning and walking off towards Avenue D. I would have told him I'd just typed William's new novel but Corso was obviously a bit junksick.

When I got back to the Bunker Jenny was frazzled. "Where were you? It's been over an hour."

I explained that things were different. "You could have called instead of making me worry. You're usually back in ten minutes."

"Sorry, you're right. I was busy ducking the police cars and looking for a familiar face. I ran into Star who hooked me up with Black Sunday."

I took the bundles out of my pocket but did not mention that I had a small Raven .25 semi-automatic pistol in my pocket. William gave me the gun when I finished typing *Dead Roads*. I'd become used to guns being no big deal in Kansas. Out on the street and going deeper east than usual, it had dawned on me that in NYC a loaded gun bought you a year in Riker's. I'd have to rethink packing it.

We got high, had breakfast, and went about our day. I sat and read the pages of *Nightfire* I'd left with William carefully because I knew he'd be reading them soon. This made me very self-critical. I'd been showing him writing for all of seven years. His expectations had tightened up since the first thirty pages I'd handed him: the play I wrote for Jack Gelber's class at Brooklyn College. Maybe a year after that I'd given him a short story. When he handed it back to me he had said, "From now on don't show me something you haven't drafted five times." A nervous laugh leaked out. It had never dawned on me to draft something five times.

The next morning Howard Brookner came by. We had breakfast at Moishes' before walking to a Puerto Rican social club on Eldridge Street just below Houston. He'd been scoring there for the past few weeks whenever Eighth Street and D was infected with police presence.

We went back to the Bunker, got high, and had coffee at the big table. It was good to see Howard. Jenny put her photos and paints aside and enjoyed his company. Howard was busy editing footage he'd shot of William for his documentary. He said there were a lot of outtakes. He was shooting way more than he could use. He wanted to hear about our Kansas adventure and had news for us. He'd spoken to James and learned that James had read the pages I'd presented to William. Howard told me he'd mentioned to William during a phone call about his movie that my pages were packing a punch.

I was now settled in at the Bunker writing station, still feeling the vibrance of having worked on the Master's magic pages. With the glow of these factors I returned to my own pages.

Only Howard knew we were back in New York. Going to the office could wait until word came down that the gent who'd paid for my trip to Kansas was done sweating. Through his lawyers he was arranging to lay a hefty hunk of cash on the US Treasury. The investigation would be dropped. So that mess was winding down. My partner and I were facing diminished activity from our accounts and it looked like we'd have to dump the office. We felt bad about the staff. They were all college kids making their way through NYU and losing the income would be painful for them as well as us. We decided to do something a bit reckless but which would allow us to give our typesetters a parachute and cash out our accounts payable. That way no one would get hurt and we could avoid filing for bankruptcy. It was painful but after a nervous few weeks we had the bucks to fold the typesetting corporation gracefully. I still had the group captain position with the Litho company and a pool of writers. But who knew how long that would last. The media world was going through dramatic changes. Pulp fiction depended on other lines of entertainment being limited or expensive. The situation drove me deeper into my manuscript. I had to complete this novel and it had to be good. It would have been difficult to stay focused without the heroin distancing me from earthly matters. I retreated into my heroin habit, my insulated writing station, and my life with Jenny, who was now my wife. The pages were accumulating. Over the course of the next several weeks unexpected events fueled my writing fever. The first was a call from Jacques Stern, looking for William. I told him Bill was in Kansas and I was living in the Bunker. I explained I was a writer, which he knew all about. I wondered how but he blew my inquiry off. I was fascinated by his voice, which contained an international inflection that reminded me of overbred gentlemen in old movies. I had been warned about Jacques but he did not sound like the mad avatar I'd been led to envision. He suggested I pack up a copy of my manuscript. He would have a messenger pick it up and bring it to his Central Park South penthouse.

The next morning I gave the extended manuscript to Howard. His xerox shop was going full blast in the storefront attached to the Chelsea Hotel. He made two copies and packaged them neatly. I found Jacques' number in William's address book but before I could call him Jacques called the Bunker.

"Have you made a copy for me? I'm sending a messenger now. Make sure you answer the buzzer."

EARLY AUGUST 1982

William called the Bunker. Without a wasted breath he told me he'd read my pages and the writing was quite strong. He asked how close I was to completing the novel. I confessed to wondering about that myself. He asked if I'd heard from Jacques Stern and I said he'd called the Bunker looking for him. William said Jacques had tracked him down and called him in Kansas. "I'd just read your pages before his call and I told him about your coming novel. If he asked to see what you have, show it to him. Jacques is a handful, but he has a lively mind and can help with money. I will alert Peter Matson to your situation. Sometimes having a contract can help get a book finished." Matson was William's literary agent.

I took this information in with the calm of complete amazement. I'd waited years to hear William speak of something I wrote with such confidence. I'd wondered if I ever would.

After that call from William, I was well-fueled to continue the novel and did my best to contrive a functional schedule around the demands of keeping a supply of heroin. Scoring made a schedule less than stable. I'd go out to score early in the morning before the police hit the streets, get back to the Bunker, and hit the pages. But sometimes police saturation had me scrambling through Alphabet City to locate a good bag. That took time and effort. I began carrying a small notebook so I could continue to work when out and about. If I was waiting for a crew to open in an abandoned building, I'd break out my notebook. The pages were now seemingly filling themselves. But scoring had become crazy and I really had no choice. If I didn't pick up, I'd be sick and unable to sit still, let alone write. I really needed help.

Maybe a week after William's call the Bunker phone rang and it was Jacques Stern. This time he was not looking for William. He was looking for me.

"I've read your pages," he opened, sounding more weary than excited. I prepared myself. "I see on the news that the police are putting heat on the street heroin crews. You fucking writers will be the death of me. Still, I feel a need to be consistent. I'd guess you're spending more time keeping up your habit than writing. Is that the case?"

"It is a demanding part of the process."

"I know only too well. I want you to get in a cab and come see me. I will call Doctor Gross and ask him to assist in this matter. You can bring your girlfriend if you'd like."

He gave the address. "It's the building next to the Essex House on Central Park South. The doorman will pay your cab."

I was a bit junksick the next day as the cab curbed on Central Park South. Jenny sat in the cab a minute while I located the doorman who expected us and quickly paid the cab driver. We were escorted to the elevator and up we went to the penthouse.

I knocked on the door. Silence. Soon we heard

a buzzing sound and the door opened to reveal the man William and Allen call "the Baron." Jacques Stern was in an electric wheelchair that buzzed as he scooted about. He had to back up to open the door. As we stepped in our eyes met. He had a distinctly French face, boyish, with longish light brown hair. He issued a quiet intensity, with curious eyes and an only slightly distrusting expression. He was slim and covered up, so it was hard to make out his form. I was told he'd had polio and was crippled. A blanket covered his legs.

"Some very strange events since your manuscript appeared. A door that never locks suddenly locked me out and I had to call the doorman to get in my apartment. All my faucets have been dripping. Fuses blew in the middle of the night and I was plunged into darkness as the fridge defrosted. Three or four wrong numbers before I finally pulled the plug on the phone so I could get some sleep. Stop sniffling and introduce me to your girlfriend."

Jenny smiled and shook his hand.

"A bit junksick are we now?" he asked, eyes narrowing with scrutiny.

"The street was infected with Manhattan South all morning. The local cops get a cat-and-mouse response from the crews but when it's M South they shut down."

"Fear not, writer. I have contacted Dr. Gross and he will be along shortly. Sit back. I will put on some tea and carve a melon."

"Will Dr. Gross get us straight?"

"Us? He looked at Jenny."

"A light chippy," I said. "If you have a codeine pill it'll straighten her out."

"Afraid I'm out of codeine. Relax, Gross will be here. All will be well. He said two hours about an hour ago... but he's always fuckin' late. Oh well, we'll just have to hope for the best. Of course, pain extends time, just as pleasure contracts time." He looked thoughtful. "The units of measurement we refer to as 'time' have been moving consistently and precisely backwards in Gross's orbit. Often in emergency situations Gross doesn't arrive until the patient is just a warm corpse." With this Jacques popped a wheelie, resulting in an about-face, and buzzed off out of the room. We heard cursing and buzzing and smashing about in the kitchen and pictures him dropping and throwing things.

Jenny was studying some artwork—metal plates—on the wall and whispered, "William Blake!"

I was by now feeling more than a touch junksick. My focus was becoming blurry. Every sound could be Dr. Gross with the Sacred Substance.

Jacques wheeled back into the living room with a tray on his lap. A kettle, cups, sugar, milk. He also had a melon and a butcher knife. Thankfully Jenny helped with the tea, which freed the Baron to hack the melon into chunks with loud grunting blows.

After slaughtering the melon Jacques looked at me and shook his head. "You don't look very comfortable. Would you like some amphetamine or cocaine?"

"No thanks," I groaned.

"I get the best coke lately. My contact is Adolf Hitler. He lives nearby so delivery is quick. He's in deep cover of course. A touch of plastic surgery has him looking like an Ashkenazi Jew and he's perfected a Yiddish accent. We never discuss the War of course. He's rather contrite and I don't want to be annoying to such a good connection."

"Makes perfect sense," I heard myself say. I wanted to add, "Where the fuck is Gross?"

"So you were a student of William's at City College," Jacques stated. "He complained plenty about dragging himself uptown to a classroom full of zombies."

"I wasn't enrolled in William's class," I informed. "My home school was Brooklyn College. When I heard from Ginsberg that Burroughs was back from England and lecturing at City, I just began auditing his classes. First one I sat in on he spent an hour on the light at the end of Daisy's dock in *The Great Gatsby*.

"Did he know you weren't enrolled?"

"No, he didn't take attendance. After the third class he wondered why he couldn't find my name in the class list, and I told him. I was determined to be straightforward and earnest. 'I'm trying to learn how to write. I'm a rapid- fire typist and don't mind being useful. I want to see a master writer at work.' I noticed at once that he was more relaxed. He said, 'Is that why you keep carrying that envelope and wanting to hand it to me?'"

The phone rang and Jacques picked it up. "Gross! Where the fuck are you, man? We have a sick novelist here who would like to get back to work. Ok, twenty minutes, ok, but please no longer. Right. Right. Get a move on."

He slammed down the phone and returned his attention to me. "I see, yes he's told me a bit about you. So, we have a City College boy, a native of Brooklyn who has good pot connections, types like a demon, and wants to learn how to write by watching a master go draft to draft. Mr. Burroughs saw you comin', hey?"

If I wasn't so sick I would have laughed.

After an unmeasured and painful period of backward moving time Jacques' bell rang.

"Try and look sicker than you are so he gives you more," Jacques suggested.

"How much sicker could I look?" I whined.

"True, true. Knowing you only a short time I must say you look like a decomposing shadow of your former self."

Jacques wheeled over to the door and threw the lock. Without further ceremony in walked Dr. Joseph Gross.

"Gross! It's about time! What were you doing, cornering the market on Horse Eggs?" Jacques whispered loudly: "He's a great doctor but an awful businessman. This is Stewart Meyer and his girlfriend Jenny. Stewart has a novel to write and can't be distracted chasing the monkey around daily which takes his orgones and leaves him with limp fingers on the keyboard."

Gross looked at me. He had a very non-confrontational manner and understanding eyes. "I see, so how long have you been using and what's your daily dose?"

"Too long, high dose," Jacques cut in. "Don't make him bullshit you, Gross. Can't you see he's needing to get straight?"

I sniffled and looked down.

"I hope you brought your script pad Gross. That's all you're good for."

Gross looked at me, making efforts to ignore Jacques' outbursts.

"Get them high, Gross! You sack of pus! He's been suffering for hours waiting for you."

"Jacques, please stop insulting this man," I let out.

"But Gross lives for my insults! He shows up late and hungry for them. As it is he's usually two days behind on emergencies."

"How many codeines would it take to bring relief?" Gross asked me.

"I don't know. Quite a few I'd guess..."

"Give the man some morphine, Gross. And some for his girlfriend as well."

"How many street bags a day?" Gross asked. "Sniff or shoot?"

"Sniff. A bundle... ten bags. Jenny maybe half that."

Gross frowned. "I have some hydromorphone in my bag."

"Excellent," Jacques chirped. "Street dope's been very strong lately and he's been using a bundle a day. I could use a bit myself," he added.

Jacques wheeled into the kitchen and returned with a bottle of water and glasses. "Stew, give the good Doctor that reefer you've been considering lighting for the past hour," Jacques suggested. "He is fond of pot and that joint smells splendid."

I removed the joint from my cigarette pack. "This is stickless Thai. Very strong. I can't smoke it when I'm junksick so I was waiting." I fired it up and handed it to Gross.

Jacques laughed at Gross's enthusiasm for the reefer. "The good Doc is an enthusiastic pot head, but rest assured he's also a brilliant shrink which is the only reason I tolerate his nonsense."

"Oh! I am sitting here with Dr. Fraud?"

Gross smiled as he rampaged through his black leather doctor's bag.

"Hydromorphone is rather strong but I'm out of codeine. We'll try 7.5 mg orally for you and half that for Jenny." Gross handed us pills. He looked up and said, "My training goes up in smoke with writers. You're not the first. Jacques has called me with Gregory Corso emergencies more than once. I'm used to divergent responses to stimuli. From here on out it's strictly instinct."

I looked at Dr. Gross with new respect. I liked him instantly.

Just knowing it was coming made us relax and very soon the shit was kicking in and I decided to be candid. "I'm writing this novel and it's just rolling along like it's writing itself. The heroin is providing a very real and useful distance from earthly matters. There's a line in *Naked Lunch* that explains much: 'I have known through faulty human equipment the vacant courage to allow all messages in and out.'"

Gross smiled. "Yes, the Honeymoon Stage of opiate addiction can be useful to a writer. I won't deny that. I've seen it close up. The conscious mind steps aside or at least stops calling the shots. Worked for Burroughs, for Proust... for many. But you must be aware of the price. The party does end."

"I'm sure... but for now I'm gonna ride it until my novel is finished."

"Not much choice, hey?" Jacques inserted, glancing at Gross. "We must help him get through this. It's his calling. The Demon will destroy him."

Gross clearly understood what Jacques was telling him and took no objection to the logic of it. I was impressed with them and thankful that my teacher had arranged for me to be situated in such understanding company.

I didn't realize it at the time, but the following months would show me what a blessing these two gents would become. Jacques was behind me now. I had access to his wild imagination and hyper-educated thought process. He helped with energy, ideas, and money. The perfect person to be around while working on a novel. The amazing thing about Jacques was how he fit into the

Burroughsian orbit. Most everyone I met through William was influenced by him. Jacques inverted this: William was clearly influenced by Jacques. This is made apparent in the first publication of *Naked Lunch* issued by Olympia Press in Paris, 1959. Jacques Stern is mentioned in a footnote as the source of mathematical theories William played with in that great novel. The footnote was not included in later printings as it was removed at Jacques' request. Being reclusive and wealthy, he felt no need to be included. William had placed me in the company of a brilliant and playful mind, a fellow morphinist, an enthusiastic patron. It should be noted that *Naked Lunch* was already written by the time Brion Gysin assumed his place in William's history, which is certainly not to be discounted. William was great at banging out material but needed help assembling his work. Gysin proved useful in this capacity, along with a few others including Ginsberg, Sommerville, and Kerouac. Gysin's "Cut-Up" philosophy allowed William to defend the non-linear post-modern presentation of his novel. But it was Jacque's wildly eccentric playfulness that contributed to William's ability to knock on a closed door and blast it open onto "colorless sheets that become flesh." Just ask Ol' Whisperin' Lou down at the Fillin' Station...

Some people are on earth to fuck you up and some to help you on your road. And it doesn't go by intention. It goes by design. Jacques Stern helped me write *Lotus Crew* and in the following months Dr. Joseph Gross helped me and Jenny survive what could have been a punishing period of addiction. As fate would have it, Doctor Gross had ethnomusicologist Harry Smith camped in his apartment and a patient living in his office. I gave him a key to the Bunker so he could use the archive room, as William was out of town. So yes, I went all to hell with my habit so I could sit and write, but I had a licensed shrink with an Rx pad spending a few nights a week in my spare room. William got a kick out of this. He knew Gross from the 1950s and respected him. In fact, he said, "Doctor Gross lacks that special antipathy for thought so common to his profession."

William and James were planning a rare visit to New York to take care of some business with agents and publishers and to do a reading. That was all I was told at first. I learned from Howard Brookner that William had been invited to read at a special event the Writer's Voice—a program the West Side Y Art Center hosted annually. An established writer was invited to do a reading and to introduce an unknown writer. Howard was in constant contact with William due to work on the documentary he was still filming and editing. He told me that William intended to introduce me as his guest reader. He and James had decided it was time to turn me loose on an audience and make things happen. Stir the shit. Get a response. They would be in NYC for a full week, staying at the Bunker. The reading was scheduled for October 14th, 1983.

The next day James called to give me the

official word. I confessed to being a touch nervous about addressing a Burroughs audience. James must have mentioned this to William because he called later in the day with some advice:

"Ok, Stew, figure you're going to read for thirty or forty minutes. Locate a section of the novel that you're comfortable with, that you can bring alive. The opening might be a good place to start, then maybe one of the dream sequences. You want to know these selections so practice reading aloud. Let your ear locate the rhythm, the pauses, decide on a peak and build to it. I suggest the classic approach, which calls for an hour of practice for every minute on stage. This will enhance your confidence and execution. Terry Southern will be opening the reading. Then I will read a short piece introducing you. How's the manuscript coming along? Is Jacques being helpful?"

"It's my primary focus now, William, and it's coming along steadily. And yes, Jacques is being very helpful."

1983

FRIDAY, OCTOBER 14TH, 1983

West Side Y Art Center, The Writer's Voice, 5 West 63rd Street.

Roy Burman, an old friend and East New York Brooklyn original homie, drove me and Jenny in from Brooklyn, where we'd been staying in a rented crib in Park Slope while I was writing and Jenny was editing the first draft of my novel. Roy was level-headed and trusted. His presence contributed to my fragile calm as the big Olds swept us over the river and uptown. Jenny sat quietly beside me looking totally confident that I could pull this off. I had attended enough Burroughs readings to know what a sharp audience he drew. Things were happening so fast. I had practiced long and hard and felt confident in the material and my ability to deliver it with drama and force.

As we curbed I saw Jacques Stern's wheelchair being pushed by a woman with long jet-black hair, wearing high heels, black leather pants, and jacket. I'd heard from Dr. Gross that he'd found a household caregiver for Jacques who could handle him.

"That's the new girl," I said. "Her name's Wendy. Gross introduced them and Jacques hired her."

"She's a dominatrix," Jenny whispered.

We laughed. Gross had found the right caregiver for the Baron. Generally, these employees lasted for a day or two. Wendy set a record. This was her second week, and she looked like a tower of terror as she wheeled him with total confidence. As they came to the entrance she stopped the wheel before a few stairs, looked around, and caught the attention of Herbert Huncke's young spirits in attendance. Cabell McLean and a new addition to Huncke's angels named Jerry obediently lifted the wheelchair over the stairs. Without a backward glance the lady in black continued pushing the wheelchair into the building. In the lobby I saw William greet Jacques. I was shocked when Bill bent down and kissed him on the cheek. This was so entirely out of character I wondered if I was dreaming.

The auditorium was packed. We were ushered backstage. William and James huddled with Terry Southern. Old hands at this kind of thing, they were relaxed and ready.

A few minutes later, walking to the stage next to William, I whispered, "I'm kind of nervous, Bill."

"Good, that's good. Now you take all that

nervous energy and put it in the microphone."

Ok, I needed management and got it. A simple suggestion invoking focus. I sat quietly as Terry told a little story about Olympia Press owner Maurice Girodias' concern after reading the newly submitted draft of *Candy*. "Girodias was alarmed that there was no sex in the first paragraph."

The mood was light and Terry drew a few more laughs before handing the microphone to William. The audience instantly quieted.

William explained that he looked back on his pages and it's clear he was describing a very specific time and place in *Junkie*. "The War had influenced everything, including the street dope scene which was quiet and under deep cover. What Stewart Meyer brings to the page is an entirely different world: an organized and vibrant open-air street market alive with activity entirely visible, and not only to the knowing eye."

William turned and waved for me to approach. I recalled his words: "Take that nervous energy and put it in the microphone." As always with advice from William, I did exactly what he suggested...

I read from the novel's opening. About halfway through I came to a sentence mentioning William: "Billie Holiday was good to nod out with, as Burroughs was good to chill out with." And that very second a blast of microphone feedback rang out briefly. I let out a nervous chuckle and nodded towards William. I said, "He's gonna swear he had nothing to do with that."

The audience broke into laughter as William displayed his most innocent expression.

I exhaled in relief and then continued reading, feeling strong and confident. I finished the novel's opening, then read two dream selections. When I finished, I thanked the audience and walked off stage. Applause put a bounce in my step. A house host announced that William would be reading after a brief break.

I sat with Jenny in the audience, catching my breath and enjoying hearing William read a familiar piece concerning the precarious practice of Egyptian Elites placing their immortality in the custody of easily destroyed mummies. I had the feeling something important had just happened but was not sure exactly what.

The reading ended. I was in a bit of a fog.

Jenny and Roy were guiding me towards the lobby. A guy walked up to me and announced he was from Grove Press. He asked if my novel was under contract. I said it was not and still needed some work. He asked for my phone number, which I gave him. He smiled and said I would be hearing from Barney Rosset. I'm sure we exchanged a few more words but have no memory of what they might have been.

We walked into a chilly October evening and next thing I knew we were in Roy's Olds blowing a reefer and rolling through Central Park.

A few days later a Grove Press editor named Fred Jordan called and told me Grove wanted to publish my novel. He asked if I had an agent. I said I'd get back to him in a day or two. I called William in Kansas. He told me to call Peter Matson, his agent. He said he'd spoken to Peter, and I should arrange to get him a copy of the manuscript at once. In a week or so I should ask Grove to send Matson a copy of the contract. I thanked William for pushing me to do that reading. With typical modesty he blew it back on James and Howard.

Lotus Crew was published in hardcover by Barney Rosset's Grove Press in 1984. Barney had suggested a change from the original title, *Nightfire* and I agreed. My faith in Barney was and remains solid. He was born standing up. He had fought censorship battles against powerful government and religious fronts determined to squash avant-garde literature under the full weight of smug self-appointed morality.

Lotus Crew was not a commercial novel and Grove at that time was not a commercial publisher. Barney pushed books he saw as important. Money was not his primary purpose. I believe he saw my writing for what it was: a possible cult novel, a tale that would be deeply interesting to the few who would get it. Placing blurbs by William Burroughs and Ted Morgen on the back of the dust cover would serve to clue the curious. I had not asked either of them for a blurb and first saw them when Barney showed me the dust jacket cover art in his office. Barney's genius also led him to place brand graphics stamped on glassine dope bags at every chapter opening. Hard to imagine what it meant being published by the very man responsible for the tattered copy of *Tropic of Cancer* I'd found in a dusty used bookstore on Flatbush Avenue as a 12-year-old. That book would not have been there if Barney hadn't gone to court and risked his life, his business, and his freedom. Barney told me he'd had a check for 100K made out to Henry Miller on his desk for a year and the perpetually broke Miller refused come by, sign a contract, and take it. Miller was sure he and Barney would both land in prison if his novel was published in the States.

There was no great change in my life when *Lotus Crew* hit the bookstores. Thanks to Ira Silverberg's gift for promo, I did a few readings, was interviewed on WBAI, and appeared in various mainstream and underground papers. The novel was reviewed in the *Village Voice*, along with an interview. Reviews were mostly favorable but a few objected to all the slang. Unfortunately, Barney's *Evergreen Review Magazine*, which he created to promote Grove Press books, was no longer printing. Grove was having financial problems.

I considered getting my habit under control but the Lower East Side was saturated with strong heroin and there I was in the middle of it. I had a hunch that the honeymoon stage Dr. Gross had described was about over, but it seemed counterintuitive to stop using. Realizing this truly scared me and triggered the original fear of heroin that kept me away from it as a teen in Brooklyn. Yes, that shit's too good to be true. I had to stop...

*

One morning I walked into Chrystie Street Park to pick up from the Black Sunday Crew. It was very early morning. The police weren't out yet. The Crew often opened at 7 am on Chrystie and switched to Eighth Street and D at 8:30. I preferred picking up early to avoid dragging ass through the Alphabet. Sitting on a bench smoking a cigarette and feeling more than a touch junksick, I was not exactly shocked when Gregory Corso plopped down next me. He was visibly sick. "There's Kono," he said, nodding towards a guy who was sitting on a nearby bench reading *El Diario* and drinking coffee. Kono was the street boss of Black Sunday.

"Did the kid on the bike pass by yet?"

"Not yet."

The kid would fly by any second and without slowing down would fling a brown paper bag at Kono's feet. A few workers would jump into position as Kono opened the bag and went to work. But it was close to 7:15 and no kid. Gregory wondered if we should just walk over to Eighth Street but I nixed it. "They will open any second now."

Gregory lit a smoke and looked down. He looked up and at me for a second. "I read your novel," he said. Silence. "Yeah, you told a story in the language of context... but a story yes... conscious mind writing..." He half-smiled through his yen. "But it's the dream sequences that got you a seat at your teacher's table," he said.

I would have told him William suggested I read dream selections at that Writer's Voice reading but the kid on the bike flew by and tossed the package. It landed at Kono's feet. By the time he bent down and opened it his workers were in place. Gregory and I were in his face picking up our bundles of Black Sunday. We walked out of the park and Gregory got into a car with Jersey plates and a blonde girl at the wheel.

A few weeks later I got a concerned call from William in Kansas, informing me that Corso was in a bad way. The Jersey girl had dumped his ass. He was in the Chelsea Hotel broke and junksick. Allen Ginsberg was paying for his room but that wouldn't go on forever. William wondered if I could go to the Chelsea, pry him out of his room, and march him to a methadone clinic. I promised I would try. Just then my friend Avom Robin rang the bell. Hmmm... Av had never met Gregory and had no idea how difficult he could be. I explained the situation and Av agreed to accompany me on this hopeless mission.

A short while later we knocked on Gregory's door. It took a while but he finally opened it. He was shirtless, needed a shave and bath, and was obviously yenning his ass off. "I can't go anywhere," Gregory assured us. "I need some dope *now*."

In the most reasonable tones Av assured Gregory that he would go get some heroin and a shirt if Gregory would agree to be escorted to a clinic once these matters were resolved. Maybe just to get rid of us Gregory agreed. It took a half-hour of dodging cops to pick up a bundle of Dr. Nova but we got it, then a reasonably nice shirt from a store on 14th Street and back to the Chelsea. This time Gregory was eager to let us in. He looked at the bundle and said, "Where's my apparatus?" He hadn't asked for a gimmick and we didn't think of it.

"Look, just sniff it Gregory," I said, a bit of impatience in my voice. Av gave me a look and I stepped back.

"Gregory, why not smoke it?" Av asked.

"Fuck that. I need the flash. I need a fuckin' weeper." He deflated and sprawled out on the bed. I picked up the phone and called Dr. Gross. I explained the situation and concluded with "We need a fuckin' noodle!" Gross was so used to crazy Corso stories he took it in quietly then said, "I'm gonna pass the Chelsea in a half hour. I'll leave it at the desk and have them call Gregory's room." A short while later there was a call from the desk and I went down to pick up what turned out to be a box of Helman's Noodles. We opened it and there was a sealed Number 25 hypo inside. Corso let out a yelp of joy. Av kicked in with a plan. "Gregory, go wash up and put on the new shirt while I cook the dope and load your gimmick." Gregory was so completely obedient I smiled. Av's reasonable tone had the matter under control. I'd seen Av do this in other volatile situations so was only a little surprised.

A half-hour later the three of us walked out of the Chelsea Hotel and made our way to the methadone clinic on 20th Street. We gave Gregory some money to get through the night. He had the rest of the bundle and a good dinner coming for being such a good boy. Before we said goodbye he asked Av for his phone number. Av wrote it on a matchbook. Corso said thanks and shook our hands before turning and walking into the methadone clinic.

"I hope you realize Gregory usually doesn't take to new faces," I said.

"Gregory? He's a sweetheart," Av decided.

I called William the next day to tell him what happened. I promised to keep an eye on the situation. As it turned out I didn't have to. Gregory and Av were inseparable for the next six months.

Av had a friend who liked my novel and wanted to meet me. This was arranged. The guy, who we called the Skipper, was a very wealthy retired marijuana importer. He had been a Merchant Marine captain, California Maritime graduate, a master of navigation. He was unique in many respects. For one thing, he was in the habit of paying taxes on his smuggling profits. At the end of a trip—and we are talking tonnage—he would figure his profits and appropriate taxes and arrange for his lawyers to present a check to the US Treasury. The figure would be listed as "other income" on his tax forms, below the legal salary he reported from his maritime consulting company. He'd filed in this manner for over ten years with between one and five million dollars going to the government. Once questioned, his lawyers squashed the inquiry in a matter of hours.

I was not shocked when the Skip and Av and a few of my old Brooklyn friends confronted me on the matter of my drug use. Now that the novel was out it would be dangerous to stay in the City. They knew I didn't make much on the book and offered to cake me up for a year or so in the mountains. Av's reasonable tone kicked in and Jenny so liked the idea. I signed off on it. The Skip cashed me up and I bought a '79 T-Bird in mint condition. We found a place in Woodstock. A year out of the madness of New York City was exactly what we needed. Jenny's mother moved into the city apartment and John Giorno took over the Bunker.

William's New York trips were just about over. He'd been groaning for years about not wanting to leave his cats even for a short trip. Finally, he was putting his foot down. If you wanted to see William, you flew to Kansas. The Bunker Years had been wild and woolly times. After a few weeks in the mountains, we started to relax. Doctor Gross never lost patience with my pattern of relapsing and put me on a low-dose regimen of methadone, tapering the dose down to bare minimum and predicted I'd get tired of it. It took a while, but his oracular insight was correct. Jenny's habit was lighter and hadn't run as long. She was ten years younger than me and managed to blow off her habit with acupuncture and Chinese herbs. While I returned to Kansas to type a collection of stories and essays for William, she'd zeroed her dose.

I pondered Gregory's comments many times. I had much respect for him and the possibility of being sharply criticized was enough to distance me from deciding what he meant as we sat on the bench waiting for the Black Sunday crew to open. Many years later I was sitting over dinner with Victor Bockris, who had done deep research on Corso's life and writing. Feeling reckless, I described the incident.

"Gregory's statements held the depth of ambiguity only a master poet invokes," I opened. "He said: 'You told a story in the language of context. A story... Conscious Mind writing. But it's the dream sequences that got you a seat at your teacher's table.'"

"Sounds about right," Victor replied. "Why does that baffle you?"

"Well, he kind of dismissed 90% of the novel."

Victor smiled. "Look, conscious mind writing can be strong, potent, competent but rarely sublime. He's paid you a compliment by acknowledging the dream sequences. Gregory knew William a lot longer and better than we did. You might have wondered why William had patience with you over all those years. Gregory didn't wonder. He knew. Leave it at that and be grateful."

BURROUGHS, THE BUNKER, AND THE BOWERY: AN INTERVIEW WITH STEWART MEYER

BY LEON HORTON

It was Victor Bockris, one of the foremost chroniclers of the New York countercultural scene of the 1970s / 80s, who told me that Stewart Meyer had kept a record of his heady days in the company of William Burroughs and the Bunker Crew down on the Bowery on the Lower East Side. "I strongly suggest you publish Stewart Meyer's *Bunker Diaries*," Victor said, "the best unpublished book on W.S.B." I was working with Victor on a long-form interview for *The Burroughs-Warhol Connection* (Beatdom Books, 2025), and with one eye on future projects, the other over my shoulder, I contacted Stewart to ask if I might see the manuscript. "I'm no publisher, but I know a man who is..." was pretty much my opening gambit. I was intrigued by Victor's words, but puzzled. How could such an important record of those days have gone unpublished for over 40 years? Stewart was more than happy to let me see an early draft of *The Bunker Diaries* and now, thanks to David S. Wills and Beatdom Books, this invaluable, illustrative addition to the Burroughs canon—to Beat Studies in general—can be perused, pored over, enjoyed by all. I am delighted to see *The Bunker Diaries* finally in print, more than honored to be involved in my own small way. Great artists are forged in fire. It is the privilege of others to keep the flame alight.

Leon Horton (August, 2025)

LEON HORTON: Stewart, you were born in Brooklyn, New York, in 1947. What was your childhood like?

STEWART MEYER: East New York Brooklyn, where the guns do the talking—Shtarks [Yiddish for thieves], Gonifs [thugs], and Goodfellas [gangsters] stood out. Everyone else was poor. I was raised in Flatbush, which was a bit calmer. Post-WWII Brooklyn was amazing. Every immigrant group that hit Brooklyn made it their home. I was a latch-key kid in a working-class neighborhood. My childhood was good. With the adults on the dayshift kids were free to play.

HORTON: How was your relationship with your parents?

MEYER: My father was a combat veteran, which amounted to respect on the street. It was a victory economy, but wealth hadn't trickled down to the salaried—which amounted to small weekly instalments, so the banks invented credit cards. Anyone with a job could buy a Cadillac, but if you read the fine print on that card you learned that through the miracle of compound interest your ass would be in hock for a lifetime. My parents were well intentioned, but adults were busy earning a living and had little knowledge of what kids were up to. I lived in an apartment building with a lot of kids.

HORTON: What were your schooldays like?

MEYER: I disliked school and cut often. I found teachers annoying and was amazed at what I saw as arrogance. No one really knew anything when it came to basic mysteries.

HORTON: Basic mysteries...?

MEYER: A child's instinct told me when you die you go back to where you were before you were born. I had no use for religious cosmologies, which tried to infect me with "truths" to short circuit my imagination, which I felt was a valued birthright and must be protected.

HORTON: Writers by default—by necessity—are invariably solitary creatures, and it seems to me we often find the first indications of this in their childhoods. Were you a solitary child?

MEYER: I augmented my real friends with imaginary companions, who I often preferred. I never had a problem being alone. Solitude allowed for daydreaming, which was my default mode.

HORTON: You have previously said that it was the discovery—age 12—of Henry Miller's *Tropic* *of Cancer* that made you want to be a writer. What was it about that book or that writer that inspired you?

MEYER: Henry Miller was articulating matters I found liberating. He was not locked into a belief system, wasn't pedantic or wedged into a structure. As a kid, it was like having a very smart friend I could invoke simply by opening a book. Miller included sex with innocent enthusiasm; just an expression of human complexity. Not a hint of "dirty" or "smutty." He clearly adored women. I can still feel how different my inner life was after I experienced that book. I became more focused on the potentials of describing human interaction without pretending to penetrate the mysteries. Just observe so the reader is free to interpret. A writer only has a few solid things to go on: props and interaction, the physical, implied, or metaphysical. Miller casually burns on all turbines. He doesn't make vertical leaps, and every sentence isn't a jewel, but he shines at character description and storytelling and focuses on interesting people. Miller is not a disciplined writer but he's fun to read and provokes thought. By the time I was out of my teens I'd read both the Tropics [*Tropic of Cancer* and *Tropic of Capricorn*] and The Rosy Crucifixion trilogy [*Nexus*, *Sexus*, and *Plexus*].

HORTON: Which other writers and artists were you influenced by?

MEYER: By then I was also listening to Bob Dylan, reading God's Cousin Gregory Corso, Allen Ginsberg, Robert Frost, Melville, Stevenson, and of course my very favorite writer, William S. Burroughs. It was Miller who led me to want to write, and William who gave me a level of mastery to aspire to. I submerged myself in *Naked Lunch* and the cutup trilogy, which I consider one long book. Fragments would pop up through the ether and I'd sense the literal under the lyrical. For instance, the line "Jackie Blue Note plays Pipes of Pan as the whole structure of reality goes up in silent explosions." That line puzzled me for months. One day I woke up and I knew! A blue note is a bent note—you don't hit the note directly but slide into it—common in the blues and blues-infused jazz. Pan is the God of Panic. Silent explosions? That implies no one heard or was paying attention. See man, the lid already blew, no one noticed! Shit man! The line was completely literal: there it is! That's a magician in the heat of a day's work, a master writer leading the reader's head to be used in a whole new way! That's a key to the potential of William's writing: Creative Reading!

HORTON: When did you first start experimenting with drugs?

MEYER: After WWII. Everything imaginable was available. I started smoking pot at 13 and was kind of constant about it almost immediately. I liked the way reefer goosed my imagination. A few years later, one of my runnin' buddies introduced me to codeine cough syrup, which was sold in drug stores. You had to sign the "Poison Book," but no one checked and you could use a fake name. A bottle cost two bucks. That shit put a real glow on a pot head but came with a warning, which made it an occasional thing. First time I encountered heroin was with an East New York black cat. He also introduced me to jazz. We bought a three-dollar bag and each sniffed half. I got sleepy and puked, which made him laugh. Once my stomach settled, I felt just fine. It was a familiar feeling because of the cough syrup. Instinct and fear led me to limit myself to pot and I avoided heroin and even syrup for a few years. Sex was the demon that demanded my focus and heroin did not seem compatible with it. The next time I tried heroin was years later—someone sprinkled it into a reefer and passed it around. I liked it more the second time but it scared me. There were a lot of embalaos (goofball zombies) wafting through the neighborhood and I decided to avoid all downer drugs, not wanting to join the undead. Besides, pot was my favored head and it was enough. I didn't like alcohol and heroin was too good to be true.

HORTON: This is maybe a bit too personal—forgive me—but are you clean these days?

MEYER: Zero opiates for over twenty-five years. I stopped smoking pot and tobacco maybe five years ago.

HORTON: That's good to hear. How much has drug use—the depiction of drug use, I mean—played a part in your literary tastes?

MEYER: I recall one day in English class—one of the few classes I attended—while the teacher was blabbing away, flipping through the textbook, I stumbled on "Kubla Khan" by Samuel Taylor Coleridge and was totally fuckin' dazzled. Then

I saw a footnote stating the work was not a real poem but dismissed as an opium reverie. I was baffled. I'd read the entire section on the Romantic Poets, and it seems the strongest entry was not a real poem. It was clear to me that whoever put forth that premise lacked any understanding of the divine nature of great poetry or great writing. The comment ignited a new interest in opium, although I understood it was the source of heroin and should be feared if not respected. I wondered if the Bible could be cast aside as "not literature" because it was written by a bunch of winos in the desert. I learned from that footnote not to trust the scholars. I memorized "Kubla Khan" and decided to re-read the Romantics on my own.

HORTON: You attended the City University of New York, which was where you first met Burroughs in 1974 when you audited his lecture series on Creative Reading. As you say in the intro to *The Bunker Diaries*, "The door opened on a living legend and a very enlightening friendship..." That's a great sentence, but what were your first impressions of him?

MEYER: Oh, I'd have to admit I sensed a highly evolved criminal mind in direct conflict with mechanisms of control and not submitting but duking it out punch for punch. That response was inspired by *Junkie* which also led me to read *Naked Lunch*. I didn't fully get it at first and walked around with that book for a good year enjoying it for the humor, the excessive funny raw uninhibited compulsive behavior. Characters appeared and exited with lightning speed: Limestone John,

Hamburger Mary, and old Whisperin' Lou down by the fillin' station. There was no attempt to be grounded or connect an incident to the previous or next. Rather than storyline, or even consistence of voice, a mythology emerges through an accumulated splattering of pre-suppositions. I began to comprehend the substance of Burroughsian myth through the accumulation of images and ideas, the way the mind collects isolated fragments of a song until you're singing along with something you're amazed that you know.

HORTON: Was he a good teacher?

MEYER: When properly entertained learning is unavoidable.

HORTON: Which is your favourite Burroughs book?

MEYER: A Burroughs page is a Burroughs page. It's all one book. If I had to delineate, I'd say *Naked Lunch*, *Nova Express*, *The Ticket That Exploded*, and *The Soft Machine* are Book One. *Cities of the Red Night*, *The Place of Dead Roads*, and *The Western Lands* are Book Two. The primary works constitute the early and final stages of William's great works and present textural changes. William once wondered if *Port of Saints* might be a useful tool to ease a reader through the stylistic transition which started with *The Wild Boys* and would be developed in the Red Night trilogy.

HORTON: In his biography *Call Me Burroughs*, Barry Miles said you quickly became good friends and that you acted as Bill's personal assistant in many respects: driving him to readings, scoring dope, running errands, etc. Was that how you saw your role?

MEYER: It's hard to imagine how valuable William's patience and guidance was to my literary efforts before Grove published *The Lotus Crew*. I was honored to act in his interests whenever I could. Unlike almost everyone in his Bunker circle, I was not from a wealthy family with an Ivy League education and a bankroll behind me. I was a City College street-kid from Brooklyn. But I had the hometown edge: I could go to my old crew and borrow a plushed-out big car to make trips to and from the airport or to readings; relaxing and painless. I had contacts for the best pot in town and made it my business to see to it he always had a stash, which was essential to his writing. I owned a small typesetting company with an office on lower 5th Avenue, which William could drop in on any time and pick up a check if he had the shorts (he always paid me back, usually long after I forgot). Long before he was spending most of his time in Kansas, I'd be picking up from his Canal Street mailbox, taking care of his bank vault, forwarding any communications of importance. I saw these duties as paying my tuition, expressing gratitude. William was careful about who he got close to, but once you were a trusted friend you could count on him to act in your interest whenever possible.

HORTON: You were part of that inner circle at the Bunker, the YMCA building on the Bowery where Burroughs lived, in a group that included James Grauerholz, Victor Bockris, John Giorno, film maker Howard Brookner (*Burroughs: The Movie*), and occasionally, god forbid, Gregory Corso. Ted Morgan called you "the Unconditional Burroughsians," which is kind of neat. Were you all good friends? Did you tick along OK?

MEYER: In that immediate circle I believe James had the hardest job. William was not exactly on the planet in the usual mundane sense. He lived in his head, in his fiction. James had to deal with business communications, earthly matters, and thankfully was good at it; clear headed and business like. If William's interests were not being respected, James stepped in as diplomatically as possible, but still, lines had to be established sometimes. The amazing thing about James was his skill at assembling William's writing. William's writing style was pure magic: on a line level, on a scene level, and he was strong at self-editing. But assembling is an entirely different intelligence. One must have the entire novel in your head and be prepared to zip back and forth through a complex storyline, remembering order of events, impacts of cause and effect. This became very important in the *Cities of the Red Night* trilogy, which involved William's most plotted works. It was James who allowed William to focus on his sentences and scenes and leave much of the assembling to the one man he trusted for it. To further your question, for the most part people got along. Allen and William might bicker a bit over Allen's socialist idealism. Giorno and Allen could get on each other's nerves over the way "Giorno Poetry Systems" record albums were presented. Gregory could needle Allen over his Buddhist chanting. But these were comic eruptions, not designed to draw blood. William did not encourage petty spats and they were rare. I should mention Ira Jaffe, who eased William onto a private methadone treatment for celebrities. Ira went through NYU Medical and became a surgeon. And Avrom Robin, who would later finish law school and become a top tray criminal defense lawyer—that's the kind of talent William liked around him.

HORTON: There were some serious artistic and literary heavyweights who visited the Bunker—you were at the dinner party with Susan Sontag and Gerard Malanga that features in Victor Bockris' *With William Burroughs: A Report From the Bunker*. Did you ever get star-struck?

MEYER: Being around William one grew comfortable with greatness.

HORTON: You were also present when Ted Morgan was around working on *Literary Outlaw: The Life and Times of William Burroughs*. Victor told me that Morgan didn't really "get" Burroughs—that he was uncomfortable with homosexuality and drugs. What did you make of him?

MEYER: Ted was an old friend of William's and a celebrated biographer. His interest and attention elevated William's stature with the literary establishment, which had long overlooked William's genius. I was not yet published. Ted understood my situation and was entirely encouraging. He put a blurb on *The Lotus Crew* without being asked.

HORTON: John Giorno has sometimes been accused of only befriending Bill to further his own career. Do you think there's any truth to that? I read that Burroughs wouldn't allow him to visit in Kansas and banned him from accessing the archives held at the Bunker.

MEYER: I knew there were issues with Giorno. Nothing that concerned me, but I was cautious when talking with him.

HORTON: You appear in Howard Brookner's documentary, *Burroughs: The Movie*, which includes the flat-out hilarious sketch "The Lavatory Has Been Locked for Six Solid Hours I Think They're Using It for an Operation Room," where Bill plays the amoral Doctor Benway and you play Doctor Limpf. That must have been great fun to make...

MEYER: Gloriously bloodthirsty Doctor Benway sure knew how to handle a toilet plunger. It was hard to look appalled. The stage blood helped. After the shooting I was outside the Bunker trying to hail a cab but they sped past and I realized I was still wearing the bloody doctor's smock.

HORTON: With some notable exceptions—Patti Smith, Susan Sontag, Debbie Harry, etc.—the scene at the Bunker was something of a boys club. How do you respond to the often-discussed notion—wrong, in my opinion—that Bill was a misogynist?

MEYER: William responded well to sincerity from men or women. Character was most important to him. He was attracted to imagination and a genuine spirit.

HORTON: Nothing lasts forever, of course. All things move towards their end. How did Burroughs handle it when Grauerholz left for Kansas? Did the dynamic within the inner core change?

MEYER: The heroin use increased and he started writing, breaking a writer's block. Dr Jaffe became alarmed and started easing him into the idea of going with the private methadone doctor he'd located. It became apparent William could go on methadone, live and write in Lawrence, Kansas. Best for the long haul and exactly what happened.

HORTON: You mentioned Grauerholz's skill at assembling and editing Bill's writing earlier, but you had some input there yourself...

MEYER: In the summer of 1982, I was summoned to Lawrence to input *The Place of Dead Roads* from William's raw manuscript into a computer document so it could be edited and presented to the publisher. I'd taken over the rent on the Bunker, originally to keep it in the family while William transitioned to life in Kansas. This made scoring dope a lot more convenient and gave me a secure indoor storage space for an occasional bale or two of pot. It also allowed me to write at William's desk, which had an air of magic.

William wanted to move the project along as swiftly as possible. He always got a chuckle out of what a madman I was on the keyboard. With Thai smoke steaming out of my ears and nostrils I could bang out a page of copy so fast mere earthlings could only sit in horrified silence: 100+ wpm with an occasional error. So I brought speed to the table and knew what a Burroughs' page should look and feel like. I got the call from James. They were anxious to start assembling and needed a cleanly edited version in computer document form. Could I get right on it? So two days after getting that call, me, Jenny [Moradfar, Stewart's wife], and our cat jumped into an auto transport car and rolled out. Two days on the road before we rolled over an old bridge into Lawrence Kansas. James set us up in the spare bedroom of the crib he and Ira Silverberg lived in and after dinner handed me a bottle of methadone with William's name Rx'd on the label. That was a relief. The bundles of dope I'd scored for the ride were about done, and I was hoping William had been storing meth, as he did in the NYC. We rode over to James' office and he set up a workstation with a window facing the main street. He handed me the keys to a rented car and told me to call him if I needed anything. Dinner with William was planned for the evening and I thought it would be nice to give him a rough estimate of how long the manuscript would take. I looked over the first twenty-five pages a bit to make sure anything that might impede progress was dealt with. This was essential for a time estimate. As a daily working pace developed Jenny took on this ritual to facilitate speed.

HORTON: Your first novel, *The Lotus Crew* (1984), a tale of two junkies and their heroin business going badly wrong in the face of betrayal, is one hell of a page-turner. Partly written in a Lower East Side street argot, I found it both harrowing and hilarious. Burroughs described it as "a superbly crafted novel that says the most basic things about power, corruption, loyalty, and the total need of heroin addiction." Authors hate this question, I know, but how much of the book is based on your own experiences?

MEYER: Most of it. I appropriated two runnin' buddies I knew since childhood in Brooklyn as the dealers: contrasting an introvert and outwardly defined type. I placed them in the context I was experiencing as the novel was being written.

HORTON: There is an extraordinary passage in chapter three, which opens with the lines "Alvira wipes the sediment of centuries off his clothes and steps into the girl's chambers." It reads like a "routine," like you were channeling Bill in a way. Is that fair of me to say?

MEYER: I internalized a major character, employing techniques I'd learned from my master, certainly.

HORTON: Why do you write?

MEYER: I write when ideas, images, conflicts, day and night dreams are firing up and threatening to cause a disturbance if I don't get them out. Over the years, I've become comfortable with Creative Psychosis. It's easier when you get a bit older: the demons are old friends, many of them are sleeping. I write because it constitutes basic function; and sometimes it's just fuckin' fun...

HORTON: Tell us about your favorite personal experience with Bill...

MEYER: After trying William's patience for a good

many years, I got a phone call from him saying, "Those pages you gave me are quite good. I think it's time for you to do a reading."

HORTON: And did you?

MEYER: Yes, at The Writer's Voice. Every year an established writer introduces a new writer and William introduced me. He suggested I practice one hour for every minute on stage and helped me select passages to read.

HORTON: I have previously asked this question of Victor Bockris, and I think it is an important one: If there is one particular thing that people get wrong about Burroughs, about the nature of the man, something you would like to set straight, what would that be?

MEYER: Victor is precisely the right person for that question. He has contributed often to important people's understanding of William simply by arranging Bunker dinners and letting them experience William's brilliance and compassion for themselves. William's work was often attacked by the mainstream press, and he could put up a chilling front. Under that was a deeply sensitive and caring old-school gentleman.

HORTON: Is there anything about yourself people consistently get wrong?

MEYER: I don't have a fuckin' clue about how people see me. I once told William it jams up my writing arm when I start looking at myself. He said, "Who's looking at you when you're looking at yourself? And just who is being looked at?"

HORTON: *The Bunker Diaries* has taken a long time

to make it into print, but thanks to David S. Wills and Beatdom Books here we are. Looking back, how do you feel about those days?

MEYER: I feel very lucky. A young man wishes to contribute to literature, decides he must experience a master writer going from draft to draft, approaches his favorite writer, and is accepted into a magical world of ideas.

HORTON: It is such an invaluable record that it astounds me *The Bunker Diaries* hadn't been published before. Is there a reason for that? Had you previously tried to get it published?

MEYER: My calling as a novelist was strong. In my journal I was kind of talking to myself. A few literary friends, notably Mr Bockris and a few writers in his orbit, were the only people I showed it to.

HORTON: We are living through some very scary days at the moment with the global rise of the far-right. Our human rights—gay, straight, trans, black, and white—are being attacked in plain sight. What do you think Burroughs would have made of it?

MEYER: William was no fan of the "leadership principle." To paraphrase: "Leaders need enemies. Leadership is strengthened by conflict, weakened by stability. The entire concept is deeply flawed."

HORTON: I heard you suffered a stroke recently. How are you? Have you made a full recovery?

MEYER: Most of my marbles have rolled back, as Dr Jaffe predicted. But as my soul sister Alexandra points out, "Marbles come and go." I'm typing

35 wpm. Before the stinkin' stroke I was banging down 100wpm with the occasional error. Walking, talking, reading and writing, shopping, cooking, keeping my crib up, requires most of my energy. Feels good to be alive.

HORTON: What does the future hold for you?

MEYER: In frustration I put aside a novel I could not tie up, about a lifelong Brooklyn friend, an old-school bank robber. I'm talking 20 years of high dollar heists without a shot fired or anyone hurt or killed. Eventually arrested and facing 20 years in prison, it emerged that he had risked his life to lead a group of office workers to safety during the first terrorist attack on the World Trade Towers. This had an impact on how the Feds saw him, and to the horror of the prosecutors he was sentenced to a mere seven point five years. Right before the stroke, I'd finished a draft of this novel but had not assembled it. That will be the challenge that keeps me kickin' up dust into the future.

ABOUT THE INTERVIEWER

Leon Horton is a UK-based countercultural writer, interviewer, and editor. He is the editor of the acclaimed essay/memoir collection, *Gregory Corso: Ten Times a Poet* (Roadside Press, 2024), and interviewer of author Victor Bockris for *The Burroughs-Warhol Connection* (Beatdom Books, 2024). A regular contributor to *Beatdom* and *Rock and the Beat Generation*, his essays, features and interviews have also been published by *International Times*, *Beat Scene*, *Erotic Review*, and *Literary Heist*.

Also Available from Beatdom Books

Beat Poetry by Larry Beckett (2012)

Scientologist! William S. Burroughs and the 'Weird Cult' by David S. Wills (2013)

Don't Hesitate: Knowing Allen Ginsberg '73 Through '97 by Marc Olmsted (2014)

The Beat Interviews by John Tytell (2014)

The Poetry and Politics of Allen Ginsberg by Eliot Katz (2015)

Beat Transnationalism by John Tytell (2017)

Straight Around Allen by Bob Rosenthal (2018)

The Buddhist Beat Poets of Diane di Prima and Lenore Kandel by Max Orsini (2018)

World Citizen: Allen Ginsberg as Traveller by David S. Wills (2019)

Burroughs and Scotland: Dethroning the Ancients: The Commitment of Exile by Chris Kelso (2021)

High White Notes: The Rise and Fall of Gonzo Journalism by David S. Wills (2021)

Thomas Merton, Lawrence Ferlinghetti, and the Protection of All Beings by Bill Morgan (2022)

The Burroughs-Warhol Connection by Victor Bockris (2024)

The Bunker Diaries by Stewart Meyer (2025)

A Remarkable Collection of Angels: A History of the 6 Gallery Reading by David S. Wills (2025)

The Three Wives of Queer William S. Burroughs by Thomas Antonic (2026)

www.ingramcontent.com/pod-product-compliance
Lightning Source LLC
Chambersburg PA
CBHW020340010526
44119CB00048B/541